Gun Trafficking in America

America

by

Michael R. Weisser

in collaboration with

William A. Weisser

Volume 5: Guns in America

Published by:

TeeTee Press
Ware MA 01082

Cover design by Damonza

ISBN: 0692386122
ISBN-13: 978-0692386125

10 9 8 7 6 5 4 3 2 1

First Edition

For Jon Galef

ALSO BY MICHAEL R. WEISSER

The Peasants of the Montes: Roots of Revolution in Spain

Crime and Punishment in Early Modern Europe

A Brotherhood of Memory: Jewish Landsmanshaftn in the New World

Guns for Good Guys, Guns for Bad Guys: Gun Violence in America

Hunters in the Wilderness: Opening and Closing the Frontier

Because They're Assholes: Violence and Gun Violence

The Great American Gun Argument

CONTENTS

CHAPTER 1

THE ATF RESPONDS TO SANDY HOOK

It was March 30, 1981, and I was living in South Carolina, splitting my time between Columbia Country Club where I played golf 3-4 times a week, the University of South Carolina where I taught a Criminal Justice course, and my gun shop where I sold Smith & Wesson revolvers to all the cops and anyone else who wanted to buy one. Smith had just started to manufacture its revolvers in stainless steel, which, it was claimed, wouldn't pick up rust in the high humidity of the Southeast (a claim which wasn't true, by the way), and if I got fifty or sixty Smiths into the shop each month, I sold fifty or sixty Smiths each month.

But on March 30 this little goldmine looked like it was about to come to an end, because that was the day President ("honey, I forgot to duck") Reagan took a round from John Hinckley, for which the latter is still doing time at St. Elizabeth's Mental Hospital outside of Washington, D.C., although he evidently goes home some weekends.

I heard about the shooting, which took place around 2:30PM, when I came home from the golf course some time before dinner. I don't recall whether I saw the news on television, or heard about it on my car radio, but I know that once I got into my house that there was something I had to immediately do. And what I had to do was call the Smith & Wesson sales rep for my area, a very nice guy named Carl Carson, to find out what was going on. Or to put it more bluntly, to find out whether Reagan had been shot with a Smith. Because I knew that if the assassin used a Smith, then there was a good chance that South Carolina Police Distributors, the name of my store located in the Boozer Shopping Plaza on Bush River Road, was going to be in for a rough time.

I got through to Carl on the fourth or fifth try. I don't think we had message machines yet so if you got a busy signal you just had to hang up, wait a minute or two, and try again. Finally I got through and before I could say anything Carl said to me, "As soon as I know I'll let you know." He didn't need to say another word and I hadn't said much either, because he knew who I was from me just saying hello.

So I sat next to my phone, watching the non-stop reports from Washington (by this time Reagan was in surgery but not yet in recovery) and waiting for Carl to call back. Every once in a while there would be a call for my wife or one of the kids and as I handed them the phone they would be told, in no uncertain terms, "Make it short." My wife knew what I was waiting to hear.

At around 8PM the phone rang, I picked it up and Carl's voice said, "RG," and he hung up. I suspect he had to call 50 other Smith dealers in the Southeast to tell them that Armageddon was not about to arrive. Reagan had been shot with a crummy little "Saturday night special" manufactured in Germany which could no longer be imported into the U.S., but there were plenty of them lying around and they could be purchased used in any pawn shop for twenty or thirty bucks. I don't remember what Hinckley paid for his gun but if I was going to take a shot at a President I'd have a classier gun than an RG. But I'm something of a snob when it comes to guns.

Anyway, I hung up the phone, lay back on the pillow and breathed a really big sigh of relief. The President was still alive, the gun wasn't a Smith, and I was off the hook. The next day I learned that Reagan's press chief, Jim Brady, was terribly wounded in the same attack and this would occasion a whole chain of events after Reagan's presidency that I'll talk about further along. But the point here is that I never again sat around wondering whether my fortunes in the gun business might be tied to something I sold until, more than thirty years later, Adam Lanza walked into Sandy Hook Elementary School on December 14, 2012, shot twenty school children and six adults, having already killed his mother, and then at the end of his rampage turned the gun on himself.

I heard about the shooting while I was in my gun shop in Massachusetts, which is located about 100 miles northeast of Sandy Hook. I don't recall whether I read about it on the internet, or someone walked into the shop and told me, or someone called me, or all three. But by 3PM I decided to close the shop and go home, both mentally and even physically sickened by the reports of what had gone on. And what did I do when I got home? I sat on the couch, idly watched the endless reports from Connecticut and wondered whether there was any chance that I had sold *the gun*. Actually, there was a little bit of a problem because it wasn't clear at that moment whether Lanza had used a rifle, a handgun, or a combination of weapons. Some reports were saying it was a pistol, others were saying it was an AR rifle, but nobody seemed to know for sure. If it turned out to be a pistol I would probably be off the hook because just about every handgun that is legally sold in the United States goes to a customer who lives in the same state as where the gun is sold, but rifles can be sold in one state to residents of other states, and my shop was not only located near the Connecticut state line, but was known as a store with a good supply of AR and other military-style guns.

I didn't know what kind of gun was used in the shooting and I didn't know whether or not I had sold Lanza's mother that gun. But I did know this: whichever dealer did sell *that gun* to Nancy Lanza was in for a rough time. And it turned out that the dealer who sold *that gun*, Dave LaGuercia, was a dealer I knew very well, because when he opened his first gun shop about five miles away from the shop he later moved into and from where Nancy Lanza later walked out with a Bushmaster AR-15 military-style rifle, Dave came to me and spent more than a few hours picking my brain about things to do and not do in selling guns.

So I knew Dave and when I heard that his shop had been the target of a military-style assault by a large squad of heavily-armed ATF agents (driving Humvees, suited up in camo—the whole bit) who tore the place up looking for anything and everything related to the Lanza transaction, I knew that he rather than me was in for a rough time. And not just a rough time, but a really rough time. After all, within hours after the shootings, the President himself was pledging "every single resource" to help investigate the crime. And since the crime was committed with a gun, guess who was going to be investigated? Dave LaGuercia, that's who. Not me, thank God.

But within a couple of days of the ATF's assault on LaGuercia's shop, the whole business began to get that rotten fish smell. And it usually takes more than two or three days for fish to start smelling, but this deal stunk right from the get-go. Even though the ATF and the local cops all were braying about how they had closed down the dealer who sold *that gun* to the unfortunate Nancy Lanza, one of the first things that started to come out was that the gun that Nancy Lanza bought in LaGuercia's shop was one of four guns that Adam Lanza had with him when he parked his car at the school entrance, including a Glock 10mm pistol with which he took his own life.

Now granted that nearly all of the human carnage created by Adam Lanza that day was the result of using a Bushmaster AR-15, which was the one gun that Lanza's mother had purchased in LaGuercia's shop. But Nancy Lanza was no occasional or incidental gunnie. She owned all kinds of guns, participated in various shooting activities social and otherwise, and, as is typical of gun nuts everywhere and anywhere, could spend a nice day driving around Connecticut going into multiple gun shops to look at, play with and buy guns. In fact, between her home in Newtown and Dave LaGuercia's Riverview gun shop in East Windsor, there were at least six major retail gun dealers, as well as multiple chain stores like Dick's Sporting Goods and Cabela's that also displayed and sold large numbers of guns. In other words, there was nothing unusual about her decision to buy a gun from Dave LaGuercia, nothing out of the ordinary would have drawn her to his shop and had it not been for the fact that she shared her home with a crazy son, there was nothing out of the ordinary that would have happened before, during or after the transaction to create any concern about her purchase or ownership of that gun.

In fact, when the ATF squad burst into Dave's shop, his initial reaction was that they were responding in some bizarre fashion or another to an incident that had recently taken place when a guy ran out of the shop with an AR rifle, having neither filled out the requisite state and federal paperwork or paid for the weapon before exiting the store. The theft was immediately reported by Dave to the Connecticut State Police, and the thief, a kid who had hung around the shop on many occasions, was apprehended and the gun returned. A more difficult problem had arisen in August, 2010, when Omar Thornton, an employee of a beer distributorship in Hartford, was called in for a disciplinary meeting with his supervisor but instead walked into the facility, shot and killed eight people, then turned one of his guns on himself. LaGuercia's shop had sold Thornton two pistols, both transactions as lawful as the Lanza sale, but it wasn't clear whether Thornton had used the guns he got from Riverview or other guns acquired elsewhere. It turned out that the guns Thornton bought from Riverview were left at home the day of his assault. Nevertheless, this incident put LaGuercia squarely into the sites of the ATF well before the unfortunate attack at Sandy Hook.

The 25-man-and-woman ATF team came into Riverview Sales around 6PM and showed LaGuercia an "emergency" revocation order of his Federal Firearms License, which meant that as of that moment he could not do any more transactions involving guns. He was also shown a search warrant, but at no time did anyone tell him why he was suddenly unable to sell any more guns. Two agents then asked Dave if he was armed (he wasn't), and a female agent, who in fact was a compliance officer from the Hartford office and not an actual law enforcement official, began frisking Dave's secretary, Randi, to see if she was carrying a gun. Several members of the ATF squad began unplugging the store's desktop computer and server, while others began examining the guns on display against the wall and in showcases arrayed around the shop.

At the time of this SWAT-style exercise, LaGuercia's gun shop was one of the largest volume gun stores in Connecticut, if not throughout the Northeast. Dave came to the gun business the way just about all of us came to the gun business—he liked guns. A self-employed retailer and auto broker for many years, the 58-year old first opened a smaller shop in 2005 about five miles away from his current location, then moved into the East Windsor location in 2008. The rectangular-shaped sales space held several thousand guns on display at any one time; piles and piles of ammo sat neatly on shelves, and holsters covered an entire wall that fit every model of gun. Riverview Sales was nothing if not an impressive retail operation that usually saw at least 10-15 guns go out the front door every day. If an entire squad from the ATF was going to rummage through Dave's inventory looking for God knows what, it was going to take them most of the night.

Which it did. And at some point Dave realized that they were trying to figure out whether there were any discrepancies between the number and types of guns in his store and the enumeration of unsold guns in his A&D. OK, now I have to call a brief halt to this narrative to explain some terminology and what usually happens when the ATF walks into a store. This procedure, known as a compliance inspection, was developed by the ATF after they were given regulatory powers over the gun business in the Gun Control Act of 1968. The compliance inspection allows the ATF to examine any federal documents that are created by the transfer or sale of firearms, notably the NICS background check form that every customer must fill out prior to any over-the-counter transfer of a firearm, and the acquisition and disposition list that the dealer must maintain, which shows when and from where every gun came into the shop and when and to whom the gun was then transferred; i.e., delivered or sold. Every gun that has come into the shop but not yet gone out should still be in the shop, which means that the ATF inspector counts all the blank space on the Disposition side of the A&D ledger, then counts all the guns in the store, and the number should be the same. After verifying that the A&D list and the physical gun inventory match up, the inspector then looks randomly at some of the NICS background check forms, known as the 4473 form, to make sure that they contain all the correct information about the buyer of the gun, the description of the gun, and the date and result of the actual background check performed by the FBI.

Anyone who can read and write at a 12th grade level can quickly and competently perform an ATF compliance inspection. You don't have to know anything about guns (most of the ATF inspectors I have met are not especially gun-literate, nor are they allowed to carry firearms while performing their job), you certainly don't need to know anything about the gun business, and for sure you don't need to know much about retail business at all. The only thing you really need to know is how to add, subtract, keep track of how many blank spaces you find in the A&D, know the difference between letters and numerals because sometimes the letter 'O' in a serial number can look like a zero, and so forth. It's not a job which requires a degree in rocket science.

But despite the very mundane and fairly simple tasks that are required in a compliance inspection, gun dealers by and large live in a world of fear and dread when they contemplate the appearance of an inspector from the ATF. And this is because the laws that authorize the ATF's activities, both in terms of compliance and more rigorous investigations, are so broad and confer so much arbitrary authority on the ATF that the average guy who owns a gun shop knows that once he gets involved on any level with this particular federal agency, his livelihood and his business are hanging by a veritable thread.

When I first got into the gun business back in the 1970's, the relationship of the ATF to gun dealers was quite different than it is today, not the least because there were many more dealers, but also many less guns and much less talk about guns and gun violence. The ATF says there are now around 120,000 federal gun licensees, but roughly half have collector's licenses which don't allow the licensee to engage in retail trade, and of the remainder, maybe thirty to forty thousand have 01 licenses—the retailer's license—of whom probably less than half actually operate a retail gun store. The rest hold onto the license out of habit or because they want to buy guns for themselves in states other than where they live.

The big change took place in 1993-94 when the ATF rewrote some rules and basically forced federal licensees to begin operating in a more transparent way, by dint of requiring that their federal license could only be kept valid if they also conformed to all relevant gun-dealing laws in the jurisdiction in which they lived. Many states and localities to this day have minimal licensing or legal requirements for gun dealers; selling guns out of your garage or from a separate room in one's house is still common in places like Missouri and Tennessee. But many states, particularly north of the Mason-Dixon line and east of the Mississippi River, began tightening up state and local regulations on firearm sales in the mid-90's, and consequently the number of FFL's has dropped by more than half.

At the same time, the number of guns and the annual production and sale of guns began to zoom upwards in the mid-90's, largely due to the Clinton gun bills (Brady and Assault Weapons Ban) passed in 1993 and 1994. Which meant there was also more talk about regulating guns, more talk about regulating the gun industry, and more visibility for the ATF. I can recall going to a gun show in Charlotte in 1979 or 1980, a time when Charlotte was called "the hub" because it was the place where untaxed cigarettes and unregistered guns were often openly bought and repacked for transport and illegal sales in the North. I wasn't on the show floor for five minutes when I saw one of these gun transactions taking place in full view of two ATF agents who, when I asked them why they were letting a couple of guys openly conduct illegal business at the gun show, replied, "Oh, we're only here to make sure that nobody tries to sell a full-auto gun."

I used to go to the NRA show every year and until the late 90's I never heard dealers talking angrily or negatively about the ATF. For that matter, I also don't recall anyone getting inspected by the ATF, or if it was done, nobody seemed to care. This changed sometime after 1998 or 1999, when I first started hearing stories about dealers, granted they were few in number, who were having their licenses revoked by the ATF for failing inspections of their shops. Having your federal firearms license permanently revoked was something that didn't happen overnight. First, it usually required multiple inspections spread over several years, so that the ATF could claim that the dealer "willfully" refused to comply with the regulations based on the fact that he continued to commit the same infractions again and again. Second, the revocation could be challenged in court, a process that often took several years until a final decision was made. And if the final decision went against the offending dealer, which it almost always did, he could have his wife or his brother or some friend apply for a new license and continue to operate in the same location as long as the guy who lost his license wasn't the "owner" of the shop.

I knew a dealer in Maryland who had his FFL revoked after a long and bitter battle with the ATF. His gun shop, which was something of a local landmark (his father had operated it for thirty years previously), was divided into several separate rooms in which one room held guns, ammo and the usual shooting paraphernalia, while the other room was used to operate a wholesale business in janitorial supplies. When he finally lost his firearms license, he just turned around and "rented" the gun side of the store to one of the employees in the shop, and as long as he didn't engage in the actual sale of a gun there was nothing the ATF could do. In fact, he went so far as to make sure that his attorney filed a notice with the ATF that the word "sale" in the agreement meant that he couldn't collect the money that the customer handed over when he purchased a gun. A year after his employee became the new "owner," Maryland debated a new gun bill to restricted the sale of some types of guns. The bill didn't pass, but it did result in a four-month stampede of buyers into his and every other gun shop in the state. My friend made more money as an "employee" in his shop those four months then all the years in which he "owned" the same space.

In other words, even though the ATF became more visible and more cantankerous at the retail level into the Bush years, it was still a hit-and-miss proposition whether a dealer would get inspected on even an infrequent basis (the law allowed for annual visits but I never heard of any dealer in my region of the country who had to suffer through more than one inspection every five to ten years). But nevertheless, the generalized fears that dealers had about the ATF was an accepted fact. I once had an ATF agent walk into my shop, and when I said "good morning" in a rather cheery voice, he answered, "I haven't had any dealer greet me so pleasantly since I can't remember when." Believe me, I wasn't doing it to be pleasant.

The night the ATF charged into Dave LaGuercia's shop, however, he didn't have time to say "hello" or anything else. Indeed, the most upsetting part of the entire episode was the fact that they didn't even tell him why they were there. Nor did they tell him why they were waving an emergency revocation order in his face, or using a search warrant to pack up and take his computer away. At one point after a couple of hours had passed he noticed that two of the agents were huddled in a corner holding what appeared to be a very serious and animated conversation with another agent who appeared to be in charge of the whole shebang, and Dave figured that they had found something really incriminating, a fear that increased when the two agents broke off the conversation, bolted out the front door and disappeared. His fears about the reason for the raid were allayed somewhat when the two agents returned after twenty minutes with a large stack of pizzas that were then parceled out to the other members of the raiding party. Needless to say, neither Dave nor his employees were invited to take part.

On January 27, 2011, Senator Charles E. Grassley wrote to ATF Acting Director Kenneth Melson that the Senate Judiciary Committee had received allegations that ATF had "sanctioned the sale of hundreds of assault weapons to suspected straw purchasers," who then transported the firearms throughout the southwest border area and into Mexico. On February 4, 2011, the Department responded in writing by denying the allegations and asserting that "ATF makes every effort to interdict weapons that have been purchased illegally and prevent their transportation to Mexico." However, after examining how Operation Fast and Furious and other ATF firearms trafficking investigations were conducted, the Department withdrew the February 4 letter on December 2, 2011, because it contained inaccuracies.

U. S. Department of Justice, Office of the Inspector General, "A Review of ATF's Operation Fast and Furious and Related Matters," September, 2012.

This report on *Fast and Furious* was published three months before the ATF sent 25 heavily armed and camo-clad agents into Dave LaGuercia's gun shop to figure out whether he was conducting his business in a legal manner or not. The problem was, they didn't tell him why they were even in his store or what they were trying to discover there. This wasn't the first time the ATF had conducted a compliance inspection of

Dave's gun business. They had, in fact, conducted a full inspection that had been completed earlier that same year, and while they found numerous errors in his paperwork, he was able to account for all his guns. Nevertheless, he was then sent a letter stating that his license was going to be revoked because he had "willfully" made mistakes in the paperwork, which meant that the ATF found the same types of errors in the last inspection that they had found in previous visits to the store. Dave had then attended a hearing at the ATF office in Hartford to plead his case and was still waiting for a final decision to be made as to the results of that inspection. But that inspection hadn't been conducted by compliance clerks surrounded by a SWAT team, that inspection hadn't started with Dave being personally patted down and searched, and that inspection hadn't resulted in his business being shut down before the inspection even began.

The next morning Dave returned to his shop to begin the process of trying to figure out how to attract customers to a gun shop which couldn't sell guns. The phone was ringing off the hook as he walked through the door; press and media were deluging him with requests and demands to talk. On the advice of his lawyer whom he had called shortly after the ATF came barging through the door he hadn't said a word to anyone, but the ATF and the local cops had already raised a storm.

Here's a story that was posted on the internet Friday by Channel 3, WFSB:

> The ATF raided a gun store in East Windsor, Connecticut on Thursday evening after 26-year-old Jordan Marsh, who you can see in the video above stealing a rifle, was found to have an AR-15 with a scope in his possession at the Hartford Hilton on Saturday. Marsh did not pay for the gun, he simply took it off the rack and walked out of the store without anyone realizing it. Marsh reportedly has a history of mental illnesses and police believe he was planning to carry out an attack "similar" to that of Adam Lanza. The gun store, Riverview Gun Sales, is also the same store where at least one of the guns used by Adam Lanza at the Sandy Hook Elementary School shootings was purchased by his mother, Nancy Lanza.

In fact the walkout of the gun performed by Marsh had occurred the previous week and the video which played on WFSB's website was a security video that was taken by the video camera inside Dave's store, which he had handed over to the local cops when he reported the theft of the AR-15. The WFSB story not only didn't identify the source of the video, but mistakenly claimed that Marsh had simply walked out of Riverview "without anyone realizing it," when, in fact, store employees chased Marsh across the parking lot but returned to the store when the thief pulled a knife on them and then ran into some nearby woods.

The Hartford Courant newspaper ran a similarly bollixed-up story about the Thursday night raid when they tied Nancy Lanza's purchase of the Bushmaster AR rifle to the guns bought by Omar Thornton before he went into the beer distributorship and began his shooting spree:

> The guns used in the last two mass murders in Connecticut were purchased at same East Windsor gun shop. Records show that Omar Thornton, who killed eight people and himself at Hartford Distributors Inc. in 2010, purchased both the Glock and Walthers pistols he used at the Riverview Gun Sales shop on Prospect Hill Road. Sources investigating the mass shooting at the Sandy Hook Elementary School in Newtown have said that the Bushmaster rifle used by the gunman Adam Lanza was purchased at that same shop by his mother Nancy Lanza.

The story went on to note that all the guns had been purchased legally, but it was now clear that, if nothing else, Riverview Sales was a store that sold killer guns. And the ATF knew all about killer guns; after all, the gun that killed U.S. Border Patrolman Brian Terry in December, 2010, had been walked out of a gun shop in Arizona as one of the more than 2,000 guns that were walked out of gun shops in Arizona and ended up in the hands of Mexican drug dealers in an ATF operational caper known as *Fast and Furious*.

Dave actually knew or at least suspected that he was being eye-balled by the ATF because of the AR-15 sale to Nancy Lanza earlier that year. This is because within hours after hearing about the situation at Sandy Hook, LaGuercia received a fax from the ATF tracing division requesting information on the sale of an AR-15, and when he opened his A&D register and looked at the requisite 4473, Nancy Lanza's name came up. On one hand, there was nothing unusual about the sale, but there was something unusual about the trace, namely, the amount of time that had passed from when he had sold the gun until the ATF trace division contacted him wanting information about the sale. Only about 20% of the 300,000+ traces conducted each year by the ATF involve guns that were sold less than two years before the trace occurs. And the average time for all traced guns from sale to trace is about 12 years. So the fact that the ATF contacted him about Lanza's AR-15 within 24 hours after the shooting was something of a surprise. And shortly after LaGuercia came into his store the day after the raid, he found himself looking at yet another surprise when an ATF agent walked in and handed him the results of the inspection which showed that the store was evidently missing 28 guns.

Given the hysteria that was ramping up all over the country, particularly in Connecticut after Sandy Hook, the fact that the shop which provided the AR-15 to Nancy Lanza couldn't account for 28 other guns was, to put it bluntly, some serious shit. The ATF agent gave the list of missing guns to LaGuercia and told him that to make life easier for everyone the ATF had done him the favor of already reporting these guns to the national missing/stolen list compiled and maintained by the agency at its complex in West Virginia. The list is based on reports from gun dealers who are required to inform both their local police departments and the ATF within 48 hours after discovering the absence of the guns, and unless the dealer believes that the gun or guns were actually stolen, they are reported as "missing" because this covers the possibility that the guns might still be around somewhere but the paperwork covering the inventory was just screwed up.

LaGuercia was no stranger to the ATF's missing/stolen operation, having reported a bunch of guns that were stolen from his shop in 2007 by an employee who later pleaded guilty to the thefts and received a sentence of probation because it turned out that all the guns he had swiped from the store were just lying around in his home. But the fact that more guns were now missing, along with the whole Thornton-Lanza business, plus the kid who had ran out with the AR-15, was enough to cause Dave some real concern. What was equally concerning was the fact that when he moved into his new location he purchased a very sophisticated and very expensive point-of-sale scanner and computer system which updated his gun inventory every time a weapon came into the shop and every time a weapon went out. Assuming, of course, that the transactions had been entered properly into the system either manually or by being scanned.

But the moment that Dave looked at the sheet of "missing" guns his fears began to ebb, because even though his store contained several thousand handguns and long guns, now all packed away or lying underneath blankets and other coverings so that they would not be displayed for sale, he recognized some of the actual guns listed on the sheet, either because he knew the model, or he remembered the serial number, or both.

How was it that Dave LaGuercia could actually identify specific guns from a typed list when there were thousands of guns in his store? Because, and here I'm going to depart briefly from my narrative because it's worth taking the reader on a slight detour, Dave LaGuercia was, in the words of one of his wholesalers, a guy who just couldn't say "no" when it came to owning or stocking a gun.

I know what I'm talking about because I suffer from the same illness, and only a lack of money keeps me from indulging in the same behavior that created Dave LaGuercia's problems with guns. Because if it were up to me and if I had enough space in my own gun store, I would own every gun that had ever been made, or at least one version of every model of every gun that had ever been made. The truth is that most gun dealers are obsessed and perhaps compulsively obsessed with guns. It's not like owning a drug store or a hardware store or even a clothing boutique. Folks who own those kinds of businesses may enjoy retail sales, and may like to see how fashions or products change from season to season and year to year. They may also like talking about certain types of products to the patrons who come in to buy.

But here's what's different about guns: for every 10 guns that go out the door of your shop, 4 or 5 come walking in. That's the nature of the gun business, it's based not just on purchase, but on purchase and trade. So in a shop like Riverview, you have to figure that if Dave sold 500 guns a month, which was probably the minimum, he probably took in 200 guns in trade, and there isn't a gun shop in the United States in which if you want to trade in a gun, the owner isn't called over to take a look at what you want to trade and give you a price for what it's worth. Do you think only the owner knows what that used gun will fetch when he resells it? Do you think that only the owner can figure out the correct markup and come up with a fair price? Think again. The reason the owner is always asked to come out from his office or someplace else where he's hiding and tell you what your used gun is worth is because he wants to make damn sure that he gets to touch and play with every used gun that comes into the store.

I once had a guy wander into my shop holding some kind of gun wrapped up in a towel under his arm. After I told him that, yes, I was always interested in taking guns in trade, he lay the towel down on my counter and unwrapped a perfect, and I mean absolutely mint Artillery Luger with all matching numbers and parts, original finish and original grips, and told me he wanted to trade it for a modern pistol and maybe some cash. The last time I felt the way that I felt when I saw this Luger was many years previously, when I was living in New York City and went downtown to an art gallery with my friend Jim Beck, who was Chairman of the Art History Department at Columbia University, to authenticate a Michelangelo. Of course it wasn't a real Michelangelo; it was a painting done by the student of Michelangelo's assistant which, as Jim explained to me, was the closest we would ever get to a Michelangelo itself.

When that beautiful, perfect Artillery Luger plopped down on my counter, it wasn't a Michelangelo; it was better. And I guarantee you that if I had taken that gun from the old guy and stuck it in my display case, it would have been gone before the middle of the afternoon. Which is why the shop owner always comes out to look at every used gun that is traded in, because if it's a real beauty of a piece, it's not going to sit around very long. Which is the real reason that Dave LaGuercia had so many guns; not just because he did a big volume, but because the more guns in the store, the more guns that might come in. And there's nothing like sitting there all day dreaming about the Python in a satin nickel finish, or a Winchester 64 in some kind of oddball caliber, or a commercial 1911 Colt made just after the War. And I don't mean the Second World War. I used to have one of John Browning's engineering masterpieces, the Colt 1911, that was made at the Hartford factory in 1920; it had the date stamped right on the frame, was embossed with the original Colt logo (which was the very first commercial trademark ever granted by the Patent Office in 1906), and still retained virtually all of the deep, bluish-brown finish that only Colts of that vintage displayed.

But compared to a guy like LaGuercia, I'm small potatoes, not even close to playing in his league. Because Dave not only wanted to have every gun model that had ever been made, he also wanted multiple items of each model. And it didn't hurt his gun-desire that he was also competing with a long-established gun shop located about forty miles away which had a very large inventory and was willing to go toe-to-toe with Dave in terms of advertising, specials, discounts and so forth. Which meant that every time you walked into Riverview Sales there were more guns and more guns and more guns.

Fine and dandy except for one thing: every time Dave added a gun to his inventory, and this is true not only for Dave but for every gun dealer in the United States, he was creating an enormous legal liability for himself for which he had no protection and over which he had no control. And I'm not talking about the liability he faced if someone bought a gun from him which turned out to be defective and because of the defect an injury followed by a liability lawsuit ensued. I was once sued by a guy who claimed that I sold him a used gun which he thought was new, and that was why the gun exploded when he fired it and a piece of the barrel ended up in his leg. It was a black powder rifle and it turned out that he had used the wrong kind of powder, but he got some money anyway because the lawyer hired by my insurance company didn't want the case, or any gun liability case to go to court. Just about all gun dealers carry liability insurance for this type of nonsense, and if we get sued we pick up the phone, call the liability insurance company and that's the end of that.

But no, I'm talking not about product liability, but about regulatory liability, the liability that every gun represents because of the regulatory authority of the ATF. The moment that a gun arrives in a gun shop, the dealer must make a notation in a register known as the A&D book, or as it is formally known, the acquisition and disposition register. The regulations require that the dealer write down, manually or electronically, the manufacturer, model, caliber, serial number, type (revolver, pistol, shotgun, rifle, etc.), date of acquisition, name, address of person or company from whom the gun was sent and, if it was purchased from another federal licensee, the latter's FFL number. When the gun is then sold or transferred out of the shop, the dealer must update the A&D register with the name and address of the person to whom the gun was transferred.

The purpose of this A&D rigmarole is to aid the ATF in conducting traces of stolen, missing or crime guns. I'll get into the details of this whole process later on, but the point is that the dealer is responsible for the accuracy of this information, meaning that for every gun there must be seven or eight different pieces of information as to its acquisition, and two or three pieces of information for its disposition. Which means that if over the course of a year a dealer like Dave acquired and sold 5,000 guns, that works out to more than 50,000 pieces of data in the A&D register, all of which must be correct. Note the terminology; not *should* be correct, not *may* be correct, but *must* be correct. And the reason I use this nomenclature is that any misidentification of a transaction might result in creating a problem in tracing the particular gun and, according to the ATF, would therefore create a "serious public safety concern." I am quoting here from an official ATF publication.

Sounds neat and tidy, doesn't it? Well it's not neat and tidy at all because I've only just described what the dealer has to do to maintain a record of the physical inventory in his shop. There's also the information that must be created, checked and maintained about the individual to whom the gun is sold. Because in order to buy a gun from a licensed dealer, every customer has to undergo a point-of-sale background check with the FBI. And the first step that takes place is that the customer must fill out a detailed form known as the 4473, on which he or she gives a bunch of personal identifiers—name, address, date and place of birth, race, gender, height, weight—and then answers a series of questions verifying that he/she is not a disqualified person; i.e., is allowed under federal law to own a gun.

The customer then signs the form and the signature is, in effect, a pledge that everything put down was true, at which point the dealer adds descriptive information about the gun; i.e., type of weapon, manufacturer, caliber, serial number, then verifies the customer's identity by noting the type and number of a government-issued ID, adds his own name and finally, after transmitting this information to the FBI-NICS call center in West Virginia, notates whether the transfer was approved. Between what the customer fills out and what the dealer fills out, the 4473 contains roughly 50 pieces of data which, like the A&D book, must all be correct. So if a dealer like Dave sells 5,000 guns in a year, he is liable for the accuracy not of just 50,000 pieces of information on the A&D register, but an additional 250,000 pieces of data from the 4473 forms which, incidentally, must be stored in exact chronological order so that, like the A&D, they can all be inspected by the ATF.

OMB No. 1140-0020

U.S. Department of Justice
Bureau of Alcohol, Tobacco, Firearms and Explosives

Firearms Transaction Record Part I - Over-the-Counter

Transferor's Transaction Serial Number (If any)

WARNING: You may not receive a firearm if prohibited by Federal or State law. The information you provide will be used to determine whether you are prohibited under law from receiving a firearm. Certain violations of the Gun Control Act, 18 U.S.C. §§ 921 et. seq., are punishable by up to 10 years imprisonment and/or up to a $250,000 fine.

Prepare in original only. All entries must be handwritten in ink. Read the Notices, Instructions, and Definitions on this form, "PLEASE PRINT."

Section A - Must Be Completed Personally By Transferee (Buyer)

1. Transferee's Full Name
Last Name | First Name | Middle Name (If no middle name, state "NMN")

2. Current Residence Address (U.S. Postal abbreviations are acceptable. Cannot be a post office box.)
Number and Street Address | City | County | State | ZIP Code

3. Place of Birth
U.S. City and State -OR- Foreign Country | 4. Height Ft. ___ In. ___ | 5. Weight (Lbs.) | 6. Gender ☐ Male ☐ Female | 7. Birth Date Month Day Year

8. Social Security Number (Optional, but will help prevent misidentification) | 9. Unique Personal Identification Number (UPIN) if applicable (See Instructions for Question 9.)

10.a. Ethnicity ☐ Hispanic or Latino ☐ Not Hispanic or Latino
10.b. Race (Check one or more boxes.) ☐ American Indian or Alaska Native ☐ Asian ☐ Black or African American ☐ Native Hawaiian or Other Pacific Islander ☐ White

11. Answer questions 11.a. (see exceptions) through 11.l. and 12 (if applicable) by checking or marking "yes" or "no" in the boxes to the right of the questions.

a. Are you the actual transferee/buyer of the firearm(s) listed on this form? **Warning: You are not the actual buyer if you are acquiring the firearm(s) on behalf of another person. If you are not the actual buyer, the dealer cannot transfer the firearm(s) to you.** (See Instructions for Question 11.a.) Exception: **If you are picking up a repaired firearm(s) for another person, you are not required to answer 11.a. and may proceed to question 11.b.** | Yes ☐ No ☐

b. Are you under indictment or information in any court for a **felony**, or any other crime, for which the judge could imprison you for more than one year? (See Instructions for Question 11.b.) | Yes ☐ No ☐

c. Have you ever been convicted in any court of a **felony**, or any other crime, for which the judge could have imprisoned you for more than one year, even if you received a shorter sentence including probation? (See Instructions for Question 11.c.) | Yes ☐ No ☐

d. Are you a fugitive from justice? | Yes ☐ No ☐

e. Are you an unlawful user of, or addicted to, marijuana or any depressant, stimulant, narcotic drug, or any other controlled substance? | Yes ☐ No ☐

f. Have you ever been adjudicated mentally defective (which includes a determination by a court, board, commission, or other lawful authority that you are a danger to yourself or to others or are incompetent to manage your own affairs) OR have you ever been committed to a mental institution? (See Instructions for Question 11.f.) | Yes ☐ No ☐

g. Have you been discharged from the Armed Forces under **dishonorable** conditions? | Yes ☐ No ☐

h. Are you subject to a court order restraining you from harassing, stalking, or threatening your child or an intimate partner or child of such partner? (See Instructions for Question 11.h.) | Yes ☐ No ☐

i. Have you ever been convicted in any court of a misdemeanor crime of domestic violence? (See Instructions for Question 11.i.) | Yes ☐ No ☐

j. Have you ever renounced your United States citizenship? | Yes ☐ No ☐

k. Are you an alien **illegally** in the United States? | Yes ☐ No ☐

l. Are you an alien admitted to the United States under a nonimmigrant visa? (See Instructions for Question 11.l.) If you answered "no" to this question, do **NOT** respond to question 12 and proceed to question 13. | Yes ☐ No ☐

12. If you are an alien admitted to the United States under a nonimmigrant visa, do you fall within any of the exceptions set forth in the instructions? (If "yes," the licensee must complete question 20c.) (See Instructions for Question 12.) If question 11.l. is answered with a "no" response, then do NOT respond to question 12 and proceed to question 13. | Yes ☐ No ☐

13. What is your State of residence (if any)? (See Instructions for Question 13.) | 14. What is your country of citizenship? (List/check more than one, if applicable. If you are a citizen of the United States, proceed to question 16.) ☐ United States of America ☐ Other (Specify) ___ | 15. If you are not a citizen of the United States, what is your U.S.-issued alien number or admission number?

Note: Previous Editions Are Obsolete
Page 1 of 6 | Transferee (Buyer) Continue to Next Page **STAPLE IF PAGES BECOME SEPARATED** | ATF Form 4473 (5300.9) Part I Revised April 2012

You might think that I'm getting a little picky when I say that dealers are responsible for every bit of data that the law requires them to collect on the 4473 pictured above. After all, what's the big deal if someone forgot to check whether they are Hispanic or Not Hispanic in Box 10a of the 4473? Or let's say the dealer described a certain gun in his A&D book as being in .22 caliber and then it was identified as a .32 caliber on the 4473—how could mistakes like this constitute a threat to public safety? Well, if the ATF wants to consider such mistakes threats to public safety, they do.

And the reason these mistakes could constitute a threat to public safety goes back to what I previously said about the rationale for the creation of this entire mountain of paperwork, namely, the necessity to trace stolen or missing guns in an effort to prevent "straw sales."

All firearms purchasers are required to fill out an ATF Form 4473 ("4473") and swear to the fact that the gun is for their own use, rather than on behalf of someone else. "Straw purchasing" is when a buyer lies about this fact. Federal law provides that whoever "knowingly makes any false statement or representation with respect to the information required . . . to be kept in the records" of an FFL can be fined $250,000, imprisoned up to five years, or both. Additionally, 18 U.S.C. §

922(a)(6) makes it unlawful "for any person in connection with the acquisition or attempted acquisition of any firearm . . . knowingly to make any false or fictitious oral or written statement . . . intended or likely to deceive [an FFL] with respect to any fact material to the lawfulness of the sale . . . ." It is punishable by up to ten years, a fine of $250,000, or both. The prison term accompanying the violation of either 18 U.S.C. § 924(a)(1)(A) or 18 U.S.C. § 922(a)(6) may in some instances be stacked for each time a straw purchaser lied.

ATF's Phoenix Field Division allegedly faced two primary hurdles in making straw purchase cases. First was the Arizona U.S. Attorney's Office requirement that ATF have possession of the gun even though it had often already been trafficked to Mexico. Second was that some believed ATF had to show the straw purchaser transferred the gun directly to someone who wasn't legally allowed to possess it. Neither of these hurdles, however, are actually imposed by the law.

First, the U.S. Attorney's Office for the District of Arizona believed that in order to prosecute a straw purchasing case, ATF had to have possession of the straw purchased firearm as the corpus delecti ("body of the crime")—even if the whole reason for the prosecution was that the gun had been trafficked to Mexico following a straw purchase. This analysis arose from an erroneous reading of a case in the U.S. Court of Appeals for the Ninth Circuit, of which the District of Arizona is a part, which merely held that when the government relies on a defendant's confession to meet its burden of proof, it must also introduce sufficient independent evidence that the criminal conduct at the core of the offense has occurred and that the confession is trustworthy. ATF Counsel Thomas Karmgard sent a memo to the U.S. Attorney's Office for the District of Arizona in February 2010 pointing out that such independent evidence need not include the gun itself, and that the Arizona U.S. Attorney's Office was imposing unnecessary requirements on gun trafficking cases. In response to questions from Congress about the corpus delecti issue, the Justice Department stated that based on an informal survey of Arizona U.S. Attorney's Office cases between January 1, 2010, and July 11, 2011, only three of the hundreds of cases presented were subsequently declined due to concerns about possession of the trafficked firearm.

Second, due to an apparent misreading of case law, some officials in Arizona believed that in order to bring a straw purchase prosecution for lying under 18 U.S.C. § 922(a)(6), the straw purchaser had to be buying for a prohibited possessor rather than for someone who also has a clean record and could have legally purchased the firearms directly. However, the statute simply says that the false statement has to be intended or likely to deceive an FFL with respect to any fact "material to the lawfulness of the sale." In Fast and Furious, the straw buyers were being paid to lie on the form by individuals intent on trafficking the gun to Mexico. Thus, the lies by the straw buyers were clearly material. They were part of a scheme to thwart the purpose of the federal regulation of firearms dealers. Regardless, another portion of the law, 18 U.S.C. § 924(a)(1)(A), makes it a crime to simply lie on the 4473.

This portion imposes no materiality requirement, and the Ninth Circuit has recently rejected any attempt to read one in to the statute. Although this section of the law has a lower penalty, the U.S. Attorney's Office could use it to prosecute straw purchasers. The Arizona U.S. Attorney's Office ultimately charged the defendants in Fast and Furious with violating 18 U.S.C. § 924(a)(1)(A).23.

Nevertheless, these two issues had historically resulted in the U.S. Attorney's Office in Arizona giving little attention to prosecuting straw purchase cases. Yet, rather than focusing on disruption and deterrence of straw purchases that ATF could accomplish without the U.S. Attorney's Office, ATF's Phoenix Field Division viewed the Deputy Attorney General's draft strategy as representing approval from the highest levels of the Department of Justice to allow known straw buyers to continue to acquire weapons without attempting to disrupt the trafficking network and interdicting the guns. In doing this, ATF hoped to be able to identify, as outlined in the draft Justice Department "Strategy for Combating the Mexican Cartels," the network of traffickers who transported weapons across the border and sold them to drug cartels.

United States Congress, House Committee on Government Oversight and Reform & Senate Judiciary Committee, "Fast & Furious: The

Anatomy of a Failed Operation – Part I of III," July 31, 2012. Pp. 20-22.

The whole point of the Brady Bill, which created the NICS system, and the whole point of the enforcement authority given to the ATF over the NICS system, was to prevent "straw sales;" i.e., guns getting into the "wrong" hands. The good news is that every firearm that is manufactured in the United States or imported for commercial sale into the United States moves from the manufacturer or the importer to a wholesaler or distributor in a legal and easily-traceable way. The manufacturer / importer and wholesaler / dealer trade FFLs with each other, a list of guns with distinct and different serial numbers is then created, and the gun has entered the market in an exchange that can be traced immediately and without any real problem or loss of guns.

But it's when the gun dealer puts the gun out for sale in his shop that the problem really begins, because although the buyer who fills out the 4473 has to state unequivocally (Question 11a on the Form 4473 above) that he's buying the gun for himself, he actually might be buying it for someone else. Or even if he is buying the gun for himself at the initial sale, he might at some later date then turn around and sell it privately to someone else. In both transactions, the person who eventually winds up with the gun might be a felon, a mental "defective," (I'm quoting from the 4473) a drug addict or some other type of individual disqualified under federal law from owning a gun. But until and unless a law is passed that requires all gun transfers to come under the purview of NICS, we are stuck with only being able to trace guns sold or transferred by dealers, hence the record-keeping requirements imposed and inspected by the ATF, hence the notion that if the ATF can't conduct a trace because the 4473 or A&D information is wrong, such errors constitute a "serious public safety concern."

So here's where Dave LaGuercia stood when the ATF finished this emergency inspection of his store. First, for all intents and purposes he was out of business. He still had shelf after shelf stocked with thousands of rounds of ammunition, hundreds of holsters, targets, cleaning equipment, gun safes and all other kinds of accessory crap that go with guns. But if he couldn't sell guns there were few if any customers who would bother to come into his shop. He also hadn't ever received a final notification from the ATF about the pending revocation of his license, a decision that had been promised but not yet finalized after his meeting with the compliance division two or three months before. And finally, he was perhaps facing more legal or liability issues based on the reasons for the "emergency" revocation, even though he still didn't know, and would never know how or why that "emergency" had come about.

The one piece of good news was that, in fact, the 28 guns which the ATF couldn't locate and had already reported as missing or stolen weren't missing or stolen at all. They were sitting on a shelf in one of the display cases, which is the reason that Dave recognized several of the serial numbers on the list, and the ATF agents had simply overlooked and not counted those guns when they were conducting the inspection and wolfing down pizza the night before. Later that same day Dave contacted the ATF and told them he had found all the guns, at which point he was told to report their recovery to the missing/stolen gun division, even though nobody from the ATF showed up to verify whether or not he was telling the truth.

That same day Uriel Patino and Jacob Chambers showed up at the store of a cooperating gun dealer with an associate of theirs named Jaime Avila. After this FFL called ATF to alert them to the presence of the three individuals, agents rushed to the scene but arrived after the suspects had left. Nonetheless, the management log shows that ATF immediately obtained the 4473s from their purchases.

Had ATF agents decided to utilize the traditional law enforcement method of a "knock-and-talk," going to the home of Avila to inquire about the firearms he'd just purchased, they would have discovered that the address on his 4473 was false, an offense for which he could be arrested. In fact, Avila hadn't lived at the address for 1-2 years at that point, a fact he would admit a year later in his post-arrest interview.

United States Congress, House Committee on Government Oversight and Reform & Senate Judiciary Committee, "Fast & Furious: The Anatomy of a Failed Operation – Part I of III," July 31, 2012. Pp. 20-22.

LaGuercia didn't hear from the ATF or any other government agency again until several months had passed and he and his lawyer came to a meeting with the U.S. Attorney who told them, in no uncertain terms, that he was expecting Dave to plead guilty to a felony. Since neither Dave nor his lawyer had any idea what this felony was going to be, nor had they been given any documentation regarding evidence that the government to pursue the case, the discussion ceased at this point.

Back and forths continued for the next five or six months while LaGuercia changed attorneys several times and tried to keep his store alive without drowning in red ink. There was plenty of red ink. Not only was Dave laying out substantial dough to cover legal costs (altogether he probably spent more than $50,000 to defend himself in this case), but every month he was forced to come up with money both to keep the store alive plus to pay off credit arrangements that had been incurred to build up a firearms inventory which he could no longer sell. He couldn't transfer the guns to his own gun license because he no longer had control over his dealer's A&D register; he could arrange to transfer the guns to other dealers but he still didn't know whether the ATF and the U.S. Attorney was going to charge him in the case or not.

Ultimately LaGuercia agreed to plead to two misdemeanors, neither of which called for jail time, but required him to forego returning to the gun business for at least five years, submitting to weekly visits to a parole officer and getting permission to travel from his home out of state (which meant sending a notification every day that he was commuting the eight miles from his home in Massachusetts to his store in Connecticut), and agreeing to a three-year probation with the possibility of fines.

Petitioner Bruce Abramski offered to purchase a handgun for his uncle. The form that federal regulations required Abramski to fill out (Form 4473) asked whether he was the "actual transferee/buyer" of the gun, and clearly warned that a straw purchaser (namely, someone buying a gun on behalf of another) was not the actual buyer. Abramski falsely answered that he was the actual buyer. Abramski was convicted for knowingly making false statements "with respect to any fact material to the lawfulness of the sale" of a gun, 18 U. S. C.§922(a)(6), and for making a false statement "with respect to the information required . . . to be kept" in the gun dealer's records, §924(a)(1)(A).

SUPREME COURT OF THE UNITED STATES, ABRAMSKI v. UNITED STATES, CERTIORARI TO THE UNITED STATES COURT OF APPEALS FOR THE FOURTH CIRCUIT.

And exactly what had LaGuercia done that resulted in the collapse of a very successful retail business, loss of employment for six employees aside from himself, disappearance of probably half-million in profits, expenditure of $50,000 or more for lawyers and a criminal conviction that required him, among other things, to appear in a ratty classroom in

Bridgeport to listen to a lecture from a Black ex-con about probation being a chance to start a "new life?"

He did exactly what Bruce Abramski did and what all the *Fast and Furious* gun dealers did on a Form 4473: he wrote down something that wasn't true. In LaGuercia's case he let a customer leave the store with a rifle without first getting approval of the transfer from FBI-NICS. Which meant that he was releasing a gun before he knew whether or not the person who had bought it might actually be allowed to own a gun. Notice I didn't say anything about whether the person who took the gun out of Dave's shop would then use it in an unlawful or violent way. The fact that someone is qualified to own a gun under the rules covering Form 4473 transactions doesn't in any way indicate what they plan to do with the gun once it's in their hands. But the purpose of Form 4473 and the mountain of bureaucratic regulations on which Form 4473 is based have absolutely nothing to do with how, when or why that gun will be used after the form has been completed, the background check comes back with a "proceed" and the happy customer leaves the store.

No, the purpose of the Form 4473 is to create a substantial amount of work for two federal agencies, the FBI and the ATF, who have been mandated by the U.S. Congress to keep guns out of the hands of people whom the U.S. Congress believe should not be able to put their hands on guns. The theory, of course, is that if guns are only owned and used by people who should be able to put their hands on guns, then we won't have to deal with the extraordinary amount of gun violence that, out of all the "advanced" countries, seems only to occur in the United States.

The question of how to keep guns out of the "wrong" hands is and has been the touchstone of the gun debate ever since the Feds got into the gun control game back in 1968. It was the Gun Control Act (GCA) passed in 1968 which first gave us the Form 4473, which had to be filled out for guns purchased from federally-licensed dealers. And since the GCA also mandated that only people with federal firearms licenses (FFL) could sell guns commercially, the two sides in every commercial gun transaction—buyer and seller—were joined by dint of the 4473, which had to be completed for every dealer sale and were then kept on file by dealers in the location where they sold guns.

I'll give you the down and dirty of how the ATF got into the gun business in the chapters that follow, so let's just say at this point that the ATF's control over the 4473 infrastructure meant that they were responsible for making sure that guns didn't get into the wrong hands. And wrong hands, according to the

U.S. Congress, meant anyone who had been convicted of a felony, or was a drug addict, or a fugitive, or had renounced his citizenship, along with a few other equally-bizarre categories which the federal government in its wisdom was convinced meant that such individuals would be threats to society if they could get their hands on guns. And if someone lied on a Form 4473 and didn't disclose that they fell into one of those prohibited categories, then the false statement in and of itself was a threat. And which agency was and is responsible for going around to all the gun dealers in America and looking at their collections of 4473 forms to make sure that these false statements aren't being made and America isn't falling prey to all these safety threats that might be revealed in an inspection of the 4473s? The ATF.

Before a federally licensed firearms dealer may sell a gun, the would-be purchaser must provide certain personal information, show photo identification, and pass a background check. To ensure the accuracy of those submissions, a federal statute imposes criminal penalties on any person who, in connection with a firearm's acquisition, makes false statements about "any fact material to the lawfulness of the sale." 18 U. S. C. §922(a)(6). In this case, we consider how that law applies to a so-called straw purchaser—namely, a person who buys a gun on someone else's behalf while falsely claiming that it is for himself. We hold that such a misrepresentation is punishable under the statute, whether or not the true buyer could have purchased the gun without the straw.

SUPREME COURT OF THE UNITED STATES, ABRAMSKI v. UNITED STATES, CERTIORARI TO THE UNITED STATES COURT OF APPEALS FOR THE FOURTH CIRCUIT.

In fact, it was the ATF which developed the Form 4473 pursuant to the GCA68 which stuck them in the middle of the gun world to begin with. Which is why LaGuercia's gun shop was the target of the ATF paramilitary-like raid, because one way or another the ATF knew that they would find something in Dave's management of the 4473 process that could be used against him. Recall that I earlier said that each year LaGuercia and his customers created 250,000 data points of information in order to move 5,000 guns in and out of his store. Which means that in the four years since he had moved into the East Windsor location his data pile now amounted to more than 1,000,000 separate pieces of information, which meant that the ATF had 1,000,000 opportunities to demonstrate that LaGuercia's behavior represented a threat to public safety, as well as a violation of federal law. And how many of these 1,000,000 opportunities did the ATF actually need to discover and use in order to shut LaGuercia down? They needed exactly one.

The data point they used involved, as I mentioned earlier, the date on which a certain transaction was called into FBI-NICS in order to get the background check completed so that LaGuercia could release a gun. The gun in question was a rifle, it had been purchased by a customer who frequently bought guns in the store, and somehow the call to the FBI wasn't made before the guy walked out with the gun. Was the shop really busy that day and maybe Dave set the 4473 side for a moment, then thought he had finished the transaction and told the customer to leave with the gun? The transaction in question occurred months before the ATF appeared at Dave's shop in December. How the hell could he remember what really took place? When he noticed the day after he sold the gun that the NICS check had not been completed he called it in and the FBI let it go right through. We all make mistakes, we all get busy, there was no possible way that because he had a new rifle this customer now constituted a threat to anyone or even to himself. But a 4473 contained one date for the sale of the gun and another for the completion of the background check, so the form was wrong and Dave LaGuercia had broken the law.

I decided to write this book because I have been following the gun debate since 1968 and it always revolves around the issue of how to keep guns out of the "wrong" hands. And the focus for much of the argument is the regulatory environment and procedures that have been developed to deal with the issue, namely, the Form 4473. In the aftermath of Sandy Hook a major attempt was made at both the federal and state levels to widen the scope of the 4473 by requiring that all gun transfers, not just dealer sales, be registered and approved by requiring the use of a 4473 form every time a gun changes hands.

Interestingly, it is during a period when the argument over expanding background checks, registered transfers and the whole 4473 paraphernalia has been very intense that very significant scenarios surrounding the use of the 4473 have taken place: the *Fast and Furious* operation conducted by the ATF, the conviction and appeal of Bruce Abramski and the closure of Dave LaGuercia's Riverview shop. This book is about those three situations, but it is also an effort to understand whether, with all the best intentions, government regulation of firearms can actually succeed in doing what it is supposed to do, namely, allowing law-abiding citizens to maintain a constitutional guarantee of the ownership of arms, while also protecting society from those same arms when they get into the wrong hands. Which brings us back to the ATF and how their role as gun regulators has developed and evolved over the past forty-five years.

CHAPTER 2

THE U.S. GOVERNMENT GETS INTO THE GUN BUSINESS

Sec. 101. The Congress hereby declares that the purpose of this title is to provide support to Federal, State, and local law enforcement officials in their fight against crime and violence, and it is not the purpose of this title to place any undue or unnecessary Federal restrictions or burdens on law-abiding citizens with respect to the acquisition, possession, or use of firearms appropriate to the purpose of hunting, trapshooting, target shooting, personal protection, or any other lawful activity, and that this title is not intended to discourage or eliminate the private ownership or use of firearms by law-abiding citizens for lawful purposes, or provide for the imposition by Federal regulations of any procedures or requirements other than those reasonably necessary to implement and effectuate the provisions of this title.

Public Law 90-618. Gun Control Act of 1968.

Notice that the purpose of GCA68, stated right at the get-go, was to keep guns out of the wrong hands, hence the notion of providing help to state and local law enforcement in their "fight against crime and violence." But the idea of using gun control to effect crime control didn't first appear in 1968; it was expressed in an earlier federal law, the Federal Firearms Act of 1938, which was built on the National Firearms Act of 1934 that regulated and basically ended civilian ownership of machine guns.

It's not surprising that so much national gun legislation appeared during the presidency of Franklin Roosevelt, because he had been in favor of strict gun controls as Governor of New York State and brought his enthusiasm for limiting 2nd Amendment gun rights with him into the White House. Both the 1934 NFA and the 1938 FFA were the handiwork of Roosevelt's first Attorney General, Homer Cummings, who less than a month after he was installed as head of the Justice Department, issued a public statement calling for "regulation" of machine guns and concealable weapons, i.e., handguns. And if there was any doubt as to what Cummings meant by "regulation," it was dispelled in the 1934 NFA which called for extremely restrictive registration of all automatic weapons along with all handguns, although the latter category was dropped from the bill before it became law.

But it was the 1938 FFA that first pushed the feds into defining who could and couldn't own a gun, thus inaugurating an argument which has continued almost eighty years to the present day. For the first time commerce in firearms required a federal license (the cost was a buck), and license-holders could not knowingly sell a gun to a felon, someone under a felony indictment, a fugitive or someone living in another state. Furthermore, dealers did not have to require proof that a purchaser wasn't allowed to own a gun, but they did have to maintain records of gun sales for six years. Interestingly, the bill made its way through Congress with the aid and support of the NRA, which found its provisions much less objectionable than other gun-control measures that were being promoted on Capitol Hill. Finally, like the 1934 NFA, the FFA vested regulatory authority in the Treasury since the law had a revenue-raising component which, it was hoped, would also deter less-than-responsible persons from getting engaged in firearms commerce (the manufacturer's license cost $25).

While the 1938 FFA removed interstate sales from the hands of individuals and vested such sales in the hands of federally-licensed dealers, the cost of the dealer's license—only a buck—created an incentive for many individuals who wanted to purchase guns across a state line to become, in effect, licensed dealers, even though they had no interest or concern about firearms commerce at all. This confusion over the use and meaning of the word 'dealer' has plagued the gun industry and the gun debate from the passage of the FFA in 1938 up to the present day. In much the same way that both sides in the gun debate feel comfortable inflating the number of civilian-owned guns because on the one hand it "proves" the difficulty of the problem, on the other hand it "proves" that guns are just another mainstream product, so pretending or assuming that every federal firearms license-holder is engaged in the business of selling guns makes it easier to argue either that there are too many dealers leading to too many guns, or that the number of dealers shows how popular and mainstream gun ownership has become. Neither argument bears any relationship to the actual state of affairs.

At some point in the 1990's, the sales brass at Smith & Wesson decided to try and figure exactly where and how their guns were being sold. Of the several hundred thousand guns that were coming out of the Springfield factory each year, roughly one-fifth were law enforcement orders that usually were shipped either directly to the agency which had placed the order or to a law enforcement wholesaler or dealer who then, in turn, delivered the guns to the department for whom they had been made. The remainder of the factory's gun production, about eighty percent of all manufactured guns, were shipped to thirty or so national firearms wholesalers who, in turn, sold them to licensed retailers all over the United States. Which meant that Smith & Wesson knew the names of some thirty customers whose orders accounted for three-quarters of the guns coming out of the factory each year.

So Smith went around to its distributors as well as sending its sales force out into the field to learn something about what and where their guns ended up at the retail point of sale. And what they discovered, to their great astonishment, was that the great bulk of their guns were being sold by dealers whose actual level of commercial activity varied between very little to none at all. Every so often one of the company's sales reps would walk into a gun shop which was selling at least one Smith handgun every week or more, and in fact the company set up a special program with incentives, promotional materials and other retail doodads for any dealer who had their guns on display and sold 50 or more of them in a calendar year.

But what really came as a great surprise to the gun company management back at 2100 Roosevelt Avenue in Springfield was how wide and thin the product distribution pattern tended to be. Many of the company's dealers were nothing more than weekend or evening operations run out of the house or a homeowner's garage that, with the placement of a display case and some shelving holding a little ammunition or a couple of holsters, were retail "shops" in the most limited sense of the word. Many of their so-called dealers, particularly in the South, were pawn shops who didn't need to stock any new inventory because the display case holding guns was always being replenished by guns brought in to be pawned. Some of the company's thirty-plus wholesalers who were together eating up one hundred-fifty thousand guns every year wouldn't ship to customers who didn't actually operate out of a legitimate, retail storefront; other wholesalers, even some of Smith & Wesson's largest customers, would ship guns to anyone who held a valid FFL. One of S&W's sales reps who worked the Southeast in the 1970's and 1980's told me it was a sobering experience to discover that one of the bigger dealers in his territory kept his inventory in the trunk of his car. You may remember that the trunk of a Chevy Bel Air or Biscayne in those days could hold a lot of guns.

By the end of 2010, one of the final briefing papers on Fast and Furious summarized the total cost of the operation as follows: "From October 2009 to October 2010 agents have documented that this organization spent approximately 1.25 million dollars in cash at various Phoenix area Federal Firearms Licensees to acquire in excess of 1,900 firearms." Despite this vast amount of money being spent by straw buyers, some of whom were on public assistance, ATF failed to confront the vast majority of them.

United States Congress, House Committee on Government Oversight and Reform & Senate Judiciary Committee, "Fast & Furious: The Anatomy of a Failed Operation – Part I of III," July 31, 2012. P. 26.

What Smith & Wesson discovered about its dealer base—very wide but not very deep—reflected one thing and one thing only, namely, that the 1938 FFA gave federally-licensed dealers a veritable monopoly over interstate commerce in guns whether they wanted to be in business or not. And this became even more the case in 1968 when the FFA was updated into a law known as the Gun Control Act of

1968 which removed the last traces of commercial gun activities of any sort out of the hands of anyone who did not possess the requisite FFL. In addition to the FFL for dealers, known as the 01 license, separate licenses were also created for manufacturers, wholesalers, importers, gunsmiths, ammunition-makers, Class III dealers (all the stuff, particularly full-auto guns, regulated by the National Firearms Act of 1934) and collectors, each license carrying a different set of regulations but all licenses issued and regulated by the ATF. In other words, until and unless a gun was purchased by a private individual, no firearm could move from any one location to another, both within a state and between states, unless the movement was between licensees granted by the ATF. If there is any other industry whose activities are as controlled end-to-end by one governmental agency, it doesn't come to mind.

And how did such a vast amount of authority over the business activity of every single gun maker, wholesaler, importer, dealer, gunsmith and collector, not to mention what takes place at the initial point of retail gun sale wind up in the hands of an agency that started life collecting taxes on cigarettes and booze in the decades following the Civil War? Because like tobacco and liquor, guns and ammunition were also subject to excise taxes, in this case the monies being earmarked for support and restoration of wildlife and conservation projects throughout the fifty states. The ATF was first organized as the Alcohol Tax Unit of the ATF, gaining exceptional notoriety during Prohibition with its Chicago field force known as the "Untouchables" led by Eliot Ness, was then given authority over federal gun regulations during World War II, and finally came into its modern iteration as ATF following the Gun Control Act of 1968.

What really lay behind this steady accretion of power over the gun industry was the simple fact that, notwithstanding the passage of the GCA68, guns simply weren't and still are not considered a big deal from a law enforcement point of view. When it comes to investigating crimes at the federal level, most of the action is under the Justice Department's FBI, which was joined as a major player in 1973 by the DEA. These agencies chase and arrest the criminals, the ATF is brought in when a federal crime takes place that involves the use of a gun. How many movies and television shows have featured the FBI? It must now be in the thousands since J. Edgar Hoover began carefully promoting the "G-Man" image in 1935. Ever go to the movies to catch a flick about the ATF?

There appears to have been a greater level of communication and coordination with ATF by the DEA than by the FBI. The DEA actively shared information repeatedly. It made the gun trafficking information gleaned from its state wiretap available to ATF on multiple occasions. Since it lacks jurisdiction over gun cases, DEA had no incentive to hoard information about gun trafficking from any other agency. Conversely, the FBI had cooperated with DEA in another operation, but did not aggressively push gun trafficking information to ATF. Unlike DEA, the FBI shares concurrent jurisdiction over gun trafficking cases with ATF, which creates a disincentive to share information and may have had an impact on the effectiveness of coordination between the two agencies.

United States Congress, House Committee on Government Oversight and Reform & Senate Judiciary Committee, "Fast & Furious: The Anatomy of a Failed Operation – Part I of III," July 31, 2012. P. 40.

The expansion and consolidation of the ATF's authority over the gun industry was not based so much on the value of regulation per se, but on the concept that more regulation of firearms transactions would keep guns from getting into the "wrong," (i.e., criminal) hands. To support this notion following the promulgation of the GCA68, the ATF created its

National Tracing Center, which it proudly advertises as "the only organization authorized to trace U.S. and foreign manufactured firearms for international, Federal, State, and local law enforcement agencies."

You won't find a single mention of anything even remotely resembling a National Tracing Center in the text of GCA68. But buried deep in Section 923, par. 3 (g) is the following rather innocuous statement: "Upon the request of any State or political subdivision thereof, the Secretary may make available to such State or any political subdivision thereof, any information which he may obtain by reason of the provisions of this chapter with respect to the identification of persons within such State or political subdivision thereof, who have purchased or received firearms or ammunition, together with a description of such firearms or ammunition." There it is in a nutshell. If anyone walked into a gun shop anywhere in the United States after 1968 and bought or otherwise received a gun, a permanent record of the transaction was created by dint of the individual filling out a 4473 Form, formally entitled the "Firearms Transaction Record," which the ATF could inspect or otherwise review any time that it liked. And as long as the dealer remained in business he had to retain these records and make them available for inspection by the ATF, and when the dealer closed down his business he was required to ship his entire pile of transaction information to be permanently housed by the ATF.

The only reason that this process doesn't amount to a total registration of all firearms in the United States is that, with the exception of a handful of states, the individual who first purchases said gun from a dealer can then sell it or trade it or do whatever he wants with it without again filling out the 4473. But think about this: Gary Kleck estimates that the civilian firearm arsenal amounted to roughly 100 million guns around the time of GCA68, a number which increased to 200 million by 1990 and to more than 300 million by the present day. In other words, the ATF and only the ATF now controls access to information on more than 200 million gun transactions, records sitting either on dealer's shelves or in their data center in West Virginia, and they have admitted that they are in the process of digitizing the 4473 data which they have collected over the years, which is a polite way of saying that they will be able to tell an awful lot about the gun-buying habits and identities of lots of gun owners by simply turning on a computer, typing a few words and hitting "Submit."

Now don't get me wrong. I'm not about to start ranting and raving about the threat to the 2nd Amendment posed by the data-mining of the ATF. In fact, on my personal list of things that might be the targets of government threats, the 2nd Amendment ranks pretty low. I only provide this information to create a context in which we will later discuss the history and overall effectiveness of the ATF. Because virtually every current-day proposal to widen or strengthen gun regulations in order to cut down on crime and violence committed with guns would involve a requisite increase in the power and authority of the ATF. So it's important to understand, from the perspective of the gun industry, what they do and how they do it.

All of this data on gun owners and gun dealers sits there and steadily accumulates to support the activities of the aforementioned National Tracing Center. The data consists primarily of the documentation that is created every time that someone comes into a place where guns are sold, leaves with a gun they didn't possess before either through purchase, pawn or trade, and fills out a Form 4473. The form contains a great deal of personal information both about the purchaser and the dealer. The purchaser has to give a full name, address, date and place of birth, race, gender, height, weight, color of hair and eyes and country of citizenship, and has the option to list a social security number, as if the FBI would have any trouble figuring out who you were without it. The dealer then has to list his name, his FFL number and store name and address, plus the make, model and serial number of the gun or guns that are being transferred, the date at which both the NICS check and the subsequent transfer took place, and an exact description of the identification used by the customer to prove that he was who he said he was on the form.

I can't think of a single other consumer item, including a car, for which the purchaser has to divulge so much personal information about himself. The last time I bought a car I gave the dealer my name and address and showed him my driver's license, which is the same type of identification I use when I buy a gun. And since the 4473 form requires that the number of the ID be listed, the ATF can get their hands on all the information connected to my driver's license as well. Allegedly all this information is collected so that the ATF can respond to requests to trace a gun that has been picked up in a crime or otherwise is the subject of interest by any law enforcement agency. But a police department can request a trace for reasons that may go far beyond the fact that they picked up a gun at the scene of a crime. For example, they can ask for a trace on a gun that was simply found, or when a gun is reported stolen or lost, or when a gun was used in a suicide, or when two parties get into a dispute over who really owns a particular gun. And what if the agency requesting this information is the ATF itself?

Let's say the ATF decides to investigate a certain dealer who seems to be selling lots of guns that end up being traced. They can send agents into his shop, without any prior notice incidentally, and look through his 4473s and A&D list for as long as they like. They can make copies of these records, go back to their office and peruse the information day and night. They don't need a search warrant, although they can easily get one, they don't need any reason nor do they need to explain anything to the dealer at all. One afternoon Mister Dealer is standing behind his showcase lovingly caressing his guns, and the next moment he's looking at a business card with the ATF logo and the name of an investigator who is saying, "Hello, I need to look at your books." Know what happens if the dealer tells the investigator that he's busy, or that he's about to leave, or that he's just not in the mood to respond to that request? He can be shut down on the spot, just in the way that Dave LaGuercia was shut down right after Sandy Hook.

But even though the GCA68 gave the ATF an enormous increase in its regulatory powers (it became its own separate federal bureau within Treasury in 1972), its tracing and inspection activities remained rather benign and limited for multiple reasons. First, it could only grab and retain the records of dealers who went out of business after 1968, which meant that it could not trace from its own database most guns that were circulating around prior to that time. Second, the vast majority of dealers in the 1960's (and continuing forward) were small operations, many not even considered to be or operated as real businesses. So the possibility that many of the dealers would actually be inspected by the ATF was scant to begin with. Third, and most important, from a law enforcement perspective guns just weren't considered a big deal. If someone committed a crime with a gun, it was the apprehension of the "someone" that mattered, not what happened to the gun. In fact, most small-town police agencies and even many of the bigger ones used crime guns to augment their budgets by routinely selling them off either to dealers or to the general public whenever they accumulated a small stash. I knew of one county sheriff in South Carolina who handed out confiscated guns as Christmas presents until the State Police reminded him that if he gave what had been a stolen gun to someone, the recipient was *ipso facto* committing a federal and state crime by being in possession of a stolen weapon, penalties for which at the federal level had been increased thanks to GCA68.

The biggest problem facing the ATF, however, was that the record-keeping requirements which they had to monitor after 1968 had little if any impact on controlling the spread of guns used in crimes. This was because the information requested on the 4473 also included the purchaser's declaration that he did not fall into any of the prohibited categories who were unable to own a gun (felon, drug addict, fugitive, etc.), but, more important, that he was acquiring the gun for his own ownership and use, and not for the ownership of anyone else. It was this section of the 4473 that was designed to inhibit "straw" sales which, from that time until now, were considered the chief mechanism whereby criminals could or would get their hands on guns. And since the ATF was responsible for inspecting and monitoring the 4473 process, this moved the agency into the whole area of enforcement as well.

But the problem which could not be overcome after 1968 was the fact that the only way that an ATF agent could learn that an individual buyer had lied or that a dealer had been less than vigilant when it came to the particulars of the 4473 was after a crime was committed, a gun was recovered, a manual trace was initiated, an initial buyer was identified, and it turned out that he lied about his background when he filled out the form and bought the gun. Because other than verifying the customer's identity and address by examining a driver's license, there was no way that the dealer could determine that any individual standing before him hadn't committed a crime, or run away from an indictment, or been adjudicated a mental defective, or fell into any of the other categories of "prohibited persons" who were allowed to own or purchase a gun.

I bought my first gun after GCA68 in a hardware store not far from where I lived in South Carolina. The owner of the store knew me, I went in there from time to time to purchase a small tool, some grass seed, whatever implements or products my wife decided were necessary for the upkeep of our home. One day as I was walking towards the part of the store which contained the nuts and bolts or maybe the light bulbs, I walked past a small showcase that contained some guns and there was no way I wasn't going to lay out eighty-nine bucks and leave that nice little Ruger Mark I 22-caliber pistol behind.

The hardware store owner glanced at my driver's license while he was writing down the license number in the requisite space on the 4473. I know he didn't bother to compare the address I listed on the form with the address on my driver's license; after all, I was a regular customer in his store. But leaving that aside, he had no way of knowing whether I was a felon or any other type of person prohibited from owning a gun. I had lived in South Carolina for about a year when I purchased the Ruger, before that I had been in New York, New Jersey and Illinois. I could have committed all sorts of crimes in those states and in fact I had a neighbor in South Carolina who while he was living previously in Virginia had shot a guy (but only wounded him) when he came home from work one day and found his wife rolling around with the fellow in his bed.

Not only did the owner of the hardware store not know whether or not I was legally able to buy that gun, he didn't care. As long as he made a good-faith effort to verify that I was a resident of South Carolina so that he was not delivering a gun that was going to cross a state line, he had done what the law required him to do and he didn't need to do anything else. If it later turned out that I had lied on the form as regards any of the criteria that prohibited gun ownership, I and not the dealer had broken the law. Which was as far as the ATF's regulatory authority went after 1968. The GCA68 also gave the ATF authority to set design standards for guns imported into the USA, the basic idea being to allow "sporting" weapons into the country and keep military guns and cheap "Saturday night specials" out. The law, also for the first time, required that every firearm except certain 22-caliber long guns have a serial number that could not easily be obliterated or otherwise erased; you can imagine how many crimes were prevented because bad guys had to avoid using guns without markings or needed to pay a little more for their guns.

The real reason why the ATF's regulatory role wasn't seen as a major concern after the passage of GCA68 was the fact that the law did nothing to prevent or diminish the transfer of guns between individuals who did not or could not be bothered to involve a dealer in the transfer at all. The law of course made it a felony for anyone in a "prohibited" category to own a gun, but there was nothing that prevented the person who first purchased the gun from then selling or giving it to someone else. What this meant was that the ATF could not trace a gun beyond its initial point of sale, particularly since in most states an individual disposing of a gun didn't even have to get or keep any paperwork from the other party to whom the gun was given or sold. The bottom line was that while the GCA68 created the federal firearm regulatory infrastructure and gave the ATF the sole role in its operation and maintenance, the degree to which the system could be utilized to control or eliminate gun crimes was problematic at best.

The gun regulatory world changed dramatically in 1994 with the passage first of the Brady Act, followed

by the Clinton crime bill which contained the ten-year
Assault Weapons Ban. What changed most of all was
the vitriolic and clamorous rhetoric that erupted from
the anti-regulation community, in particular the NRA,
which had played a rather quiet, passive and somewhat
conciliatory role in the debates that led up to GCA68.
The change in attitudes was largely a function of the
appearance of a new generation of NRA leaders who
viewed both pieces of legislation as moving America
towards the gun-free environment of other advanced
Western states. So while the debate over GCA68 had
focused on simply creating an end-to-end regulatory
framework which the NRA in principle supported, at
least in a benign form, the debate in 1993-94 took on
overtones of fear and paranoia that any increase in
regulatory activity would result in a complete loss of
2nd Amendment rights for all. The NRA's opposition
to the 1994 laws was also a carefully calculated attempt
to become a much more politically partisan
organization in which gun control, like abortion and
public prayer, would become another "wedge" issue,
that would be used to make the NRA an important
resource for conservative political campaigns. I
remember going to the NRA national meeting in 1980,
and while the tone and flavor reflected the
overwhelmingly small-town, Southern roots of a
majority of the members (this meeting happened to be

held in Philadelphia), there was very little overt or strident politics seen in exhibits or heard in the hall. When I went to the 1995 meeting in Phoenix there were anti-Clinton posters, placards and vehement speeches galore.

Much of the anger was aimed at the Assault Weapons Ban, which, for the first time since the 1934 National Firearms Act, made the federal government the unquestioned arbiter over what types of weapons Americans could buy or own. The NFA did not arouse a lot of opposition, because it was pretty hard to argue against the idea that the ownership of fully automatic weapons needed to be tightly controlled. And the licensing and registration procedures that were imposed both on dealers and automatic gun owners, regulations not that different from ownership regulations that applied to all firearms in other Western countries, had proven to be extremely effective in taking machine guns off the streets.

In the case of the 1994 Assault Weapons Ban, however, the opposition was bitter and intense, because even though it was argued that hi-capacity, military-style rifles could inflict quick and serious damage, the fact is that semi-automatic rifles, no matter what their style, had been around for more than fifty years, so it was pretty difficult to hold to the idea that all of a sudden they constituted such a big threat. I'm not sure the ban would have been enacted had Clinton not cleverly stuck it into his crime bill, the largest and most expensive piece of crime legislation ever passed. And although the NRA achieved a partial victory by getting the ban enacted on a temporary ten-year basis, the fact that the law contained money that allowed nearly 100,000 cops to be hired in jurisdictions all over the United States represented a level of influence and power against which the NRA and its allies couldn't compete. Twenty years later, following Sandy Hook when Obama tried to push through his gun bill, the fact that he couldn't come up with some kind of fiscal sweetener probably doomed the measure from the start.

The battle over the new gun laws in 1993-94 may have resulted in compromises that made the regulatory system much less comprehensive than the Clinton administration had desired, but the post-Brady environment nevertheless resulted in a further expansion of ATF's role in the federal oversight of guns. The two major flaws that came out of GCA68 were that dealers had no way of verifying that they were, indeed, selling a gun to an individual who was not a "prohibited" person as defined by federal law, and its failure to address the issue of private gun transfers between individuals outside a dealer's purview or control. While the latter issue did not change as a result of Brady, the law made a major change in whether guns would get into the wrong hands at the initial point of sale by establishing a required background check to be conducted between every dealer and a phone (later internet) bank of investigators trained and managed by the FBI.

This system, known as the National Instant Check System (NICS) began operating in 1995 and was more or less fully operational by the end of 1998. What it amounted to was the requirement that the personal identifiers given by a purchaser on the 4473 (name, address, etc.) be transmitted to an FBI examiner who would then scan databases containing state-level court records covering felonies, mental illness, etc., in other words, all the legal/penal information that might contain mention of persons who were prohibited from owning guns. The database was hardly complete in 1994 and still has gaps in it to this day, but at least there was now some kind of system to verify that what a gun buyer said about himself was actually true. And while the background check system brought the FBI into the regulatory game alongside the ATF, it was the latter agency that was given authority to deal with any issues about gun transfers that might arise as a result of background checks. In particular, in conducting dealer compliance inspections, the ATF would now focus on that part of the 4473 form which contained information about the conduct and result of the NICS itself.

The way it works is that after a customer purchases a gun and fills out the 4473, the dealer sends the information down to the FBI and waits, usually very briefly, for the result. The FBI responds by telling the dealer either to "proceed," "delay" or "deny." If the response is to proceed, the sale completes and the customer takes the gun (*or guns*) and walks out of the store (the issue of how many guns is covered by one background check will be addressed shortly and is a paramount issue for the remainder of this book). If the FBI issues a "delay" response, the dealer normally must hold the gun for three business days following the initial date of sale, and if, during that period, the dealer receives a "proceed" or a "deny" from the FBI, he must act accordingly. But if there is no response, the dealer can release the gun using his own judgment as to whether the customer does, in fact, meet the legal criteria for gun ownership.

In addition to containing the personal identifiers of the gun buyer that are transmitted to the FBI, the 4473 also contains a section that covers the actual background check process itself. First the buyer signs and dates the form, then the dealer dates the transmission of the information to NICS and the result and then dates and sign the form when the transaction and the NICS check has been completed. The dealer also describes the make, type and caliber of weapon that is being transferred, although NICS is only told that the transaction involves either a handgun, a long gun or both. There is no maximum number of guns that can be transferred for any specific NICS check; the qualifications of the buyer are of concern to the FBI, not the type or numbers of weapons being transferred.

But here is where the ATF gets back into the act big-time. First of all, the 4473 form is their form; the ATF creates the form, revises the form on occasion (they recently added the White and non-White Hispanic categories to conform to Census nomenclature), issues rulings and guidelines for using the form and, most importantly, inspects the form to make sure that all the required information about the NICS check has been entered correctly. In other words, the FBI conducts the NICS check solely for the purpose of making sure that all dealer transfers take place in a manner that will keep guns from getting into "prohibited" hands, but it is the ATF that manages the system. And this management takes place at the dealer's point of sale through the ATF's authority to inspect the paperwork created by GCA68, followed by the Brady bill of 1994.

I mentioned above that the FBI conducts its background check knowing only that the gun buyer is receiving either a handgun, a long gun or both. In fact, unless a state or locality sets a maximum limit for the number of guns that can be transferred at any one time (no such state or locality comes to mind), no federal law prohibits the transfer at one time of any number of guns, as long as the buyer meets the legal qualifications for gun ownership. Federal law does require that a dealer must report the purchase of two or more handguns by the same individual within any five-day period, issuing a form that is sent at the time of purchase to the ATF. In theory, this documentation alerts the ATF to the fact that someone is stocking up on multiple handguns, but it's almost a law without actually being a law because there is nothing that stops someone from going around to different shops on the same day and purchasing a single gun in each shop. Whether such purchases would alert someone at FBI-NICS to contact ATF because each of the purchases would require a background check is a procedure that may exist in theory but I doubt exists in fact. Nevertheless, like the information on the 4473 about the background check, the multiple-gun purchase is another procedure (with a requisite form) that is part of the ATF regulatory arsenal and it will also become an important part of the *Fast and Furious* story later on.

Not only did the Brady law increase the scope of the ATF's regulatory authority, but the debate that swirled around the passage of this law and the Assault Weapons Ban increased the visibility of the ATF because, for the first time, the whole issue of gun ownership became a much more concerning problem in the public and media arena, with a consequent increase not only in the noise level of the debate itself, but in the size and activity of advocacy organizations on both sides. The issue of gun ownership became intensely debated following an event on April 20, 1999, when two students walked into their high school in Littleton, just outside Denver, and opened up with shotguns and pistols, eventually killing 12 students and a teacher, wounding another 21 students and staff and then turning the guns on themselves.

If anything, the Columbine shooting pushed the two sides of the gun debate further apart both in terms of the rhetoric employed to describe the threat of gun violence, as well as in the solutions that were advanced to respond to the problem. For the NRA and other promoters of gun ownership the answer lay in stronger enforcement of current laws, both laws covering penalties imposed for using guns in crimes and laws that defined who could legally own guns (which amounted to the same thing since illegal possession of a weapon is, in and of itself, a crime).

For the anti-gun advocates, the answer to the problem lay in reducing the number of guns, or at least reducing the number and availability of guns that could be used in the most violent crimes; i.e., high-capacity handguns and military-style ("assault") rifles.

The anti-gun advocates won a partial victory in 1994 with the Assault Weapons Ban, but it was a ten-year prohibition, the law was due to expire in 2004 and the Bush Administration gave signals right from the git-go that they would not attempt to extend it. On the other hand, GCA68 had also created another area of ATF activity concerning the import of guns into the United States, which gave the agency the authority to determine what types of guns could enter the country for commercial purposes. This was the law that prohibited the import of cheap handguns, known as "Saturday night specials," but a less-noticed part of the law also gave ATF the authority to determine whether a long gun was designed for "sporting" purposes, as opposed to non-sporting purposes, aka assault rifles. And the ban on military-style imports, which had been strengthened under the Bush I administration, effectively closed the door on what was becoming a lucrative trade in older, surplus military rifles that were sitting around, moldering in arsenals all over Europe.

Ultimately the ATF decided that any bolt-action rifle, even if manufactured and used only by a military unit, qualified as a "sporting" gun and could be imported and sold in the United States. And there were literally millions of these old junkers that came into the country from various Western countries, a tide that became much larger when the Iron Curtain collapsed and many more arsenal imports started coming in from Russia and the former satellite states. The guns were cheap, there was plenty of surplus ammo lying around that could also be brought in, and when such guns were "sporterized" by tuning the triggers and polishing the barrels, they made decent hunting or target guns at a fraction of the cost of a Winchester 70 or a Remington 700.

The ATF also decided, no doubt responding to political realities in Washington, that semi-automatic, military-style rifles which could take hi-capacity magazines were *verboten* because they didn't meet the criteria for sporting use. In particular, the ban on such guns was designed to stem the flow of surplus AK-47s, which could be altered from full-auto to semi-auto function by changing one internal part, a mechanical fix that could be accomplished in about 30 seconds with a screwdriver and a small wrench. The beauty of the AK was that it fired a 30-caliber shell (as opposed to the AR which takes a much smaller, 22-caliber round), its functioning was impervious to water, dirt or rust, and most of all, it always worked. Like a Timex, it took a licking and kept on ticking.

Once the ban on importing assault rifles was made permanent, gun importers began to figure out how to get around the ban, and they did so in the same way that they had gotten around the import ban on small handguns, namely, by disassembling the guns overseas, importing the different gun parts and assembling the finished weapon over here. Over the years a cat-and-mouse exercise took place between these importers and the ATF, with the latter attempting to control the import of individual gun parts and the former either renaming the parts so they could be imported as machine parts that had nothing to do with guns, or importing some of the parts while making the remaining parts over here. In 1993 the ATF published an order that restricted the assembly of assault rifles if the gun contained 10 or more imported parts, and if you look up 27 CFR 478.39 in the Federal Register for July 29, 1993, you'll find a complete list of every part required to build an AK-47, so just take your pick of the 9 parts you want to import, find supplies for the rest over here and get to work.

The company which specialized in bringing in surplus military arms and either re-selling them "as is" or reassembling them from parts is an outfit called

Century Arms that used to be located in New Hampshire but now operates out of Florida in the seaside resort town of Delray Beach. In 1992-93 nearly 3 million rifles were imported into the U.S., largely in anticipation of the Assault Weapons Ban, which was twice as many rifles as were manufactured here in those same two years. I have no idea how many of those guns were brought in by Century, but I'll bet they accounted for a fair share. In the years directly following the 1994 import ban, the number of imported rifles brought in each year fell to less than 300,000, but many more AKs continued to be assembled out of imported and domestic parts.

Once an AK or other assault rifle hit the consumer market, the chances of controlling its distribution or movement beyond the initial point of sale was nil. This was because rifles, as opposed to pistols and revolvers, could not only be purchased by anyone over the age of 18 (whereas handgun sales were restricted to persons over the age of 21), but could be bought in one state by residents of another. The "contiguous state" law, which was one of the pro-gun modifications of Brady, allowed residents of any particular state to cross into a bordering state, purchase and undergo the NICS in the latter jurisdiction, then bring the gun back to his state of residence without doing any additional paperwork or registration of the weapon. Furthermore, the requirement that dealers report sales of multiple handguns did not apply to long guns, no matter how many were purchased in any particular sale. And since NICS didn't cover private gun transactions of any sort, this meant that legally-purchased rifles could flow from the legal to the illegal market without any real constraints at all. Keep this issue in mind as we move into a more detailed discussion about *Fast and Furious* in the chapters to come.

Where does this leave us with reference to the activities and authority of the ATF? First and foremost, since virtually everything having to do with guns—manufacture, import, sales, ownership—is regulated in one way or another by GCA68 and Brady, by definition this means tons of paperwork generated and managed by what is the only federal agency responsible for the oversight of guns. How much paperwork are we talking about? To begin with, every single firearm that can be purchased in the United States must have a distinct serial number and a record of that serial number must be available for inspection by the ATF. In 2012 this covered 4,844,590 imported weapons, 8,578,610 domestically-manufactured weapons and roughly 400,000 NFA guns (full-auto weapons); in other words, about 14 million records of individual guns. Along with serial numbers, these records must also identify the type of weapon, the caliber and, in the case of imports, the length of the barrel.

While domestic manufacturers of commercial firearms (usually referred to as GCA68 guns) do not need to report manufacturing activity before the guns are produced, importers and NFA manufacturers must apply for and receive ATF approval for every gun they intend to import or make. This amounted to more than 1 million NFA purchase and/or transfer of weapons and various accessories (silencers in particular) and more than 10,000 applications to import weapons, although the import applications are usually submitted for shipments comprised of multiple guns rather than for individual gun imports; hence, the much larger number of NFA permits even though the number of actual commercial guns imported far outstrips the number of NFA weapons bought and sold. The bottom line is that we are now above 15 million pieces of documentation and that's before a single one of these guns has actually been put out in some gun shop for commercial sale. Assuming that at least 80% of the guns that are produced or imported into the US are sold within 12 months after they hit the market (an assumption based on my retailing plus knowing the ins and outs of other shops in which gun inventory usually turns 4-5 times per year), these sales create an additional 14 million 4473 forms, hundreds of thousands of multiple handgun purchase forms (known as the 3310), and, of course, the ubiquitous A&D books list which must be kept by everyone who buys or sells guns.

When all is said and done, while the ATF calls itself a law enforcement agency and since 2002 has been part of the Justice Department which oversees the bulk of federal law enforcement, what it primarily enforces is the accuracy of paperwork, as opposed to going after bad guys who commit real crimes. All of the forms that are used to record manufacturing, importing, transferring and purchasing of firearms carry legal sanctions if they are willfully and incorrectly filled out, particularly if there is an intent to deceive the government in terms of what will eventually happen to the gun. But when someone claims he is purchasing a gun for himself, then turns around and gives or sells the gun to someone else who uses that gun to commit a crime, the latter individual will be charged with the crime that was committed, while the former can only be charged with lying on a federal form. There are no criminal statutes that can be applied to someone who consciously moves a gun from legal into illegal hands; the whole notion of "gun-running," which is a staple of the rhetorical arsenal of gun advocates on both sides, is a convenient metaphor for illegal gun commerce, but it has no statutory reality at all. In the various reports and press releases that the ATF issues, they frequently refer to thousands of gun crimes for which they "recommend" prosecution each year. But what they don't tell you is that virtually all of these charges are secondary to a primary criminal offense in which an illegal gun just happened to be involved as well. When the local cops arrest some idiot for holding up a convenience store and also grab his gun, they sometimes run a trace through the ATF whose vaunted National Tracing Center may then perhaps shed some light on the origins of the weapon and for sure will be able to state whether the idiot in question was legally able to own a gun. Such a trace then becomes part of the case record that the police forward to the DA and—*voila!*—the ATF has recommended prosecution for illegal possession of the gun.

The "weak sister" status of the ATF in federal law enforcement circles can best be understood, however, with reference to the one type of information which is always the best way to understand what any agency does, namely, the size of its annual budget and how the money is spent. The Department of Justice lists five law enforcement agencies operating under its purview, and their 2013 budget allocations (in millions of dollars) look like this:

FBI	$8,347
Bureau of Prisons	$6,894
Marshals Service	$2,668
DEA	$2,118
ATF	$1,201

Not a big chunk. And it gets a lot smaller when we look at how their money is divided up between law enforcement on the one hand and compliance on the other. According to the 2013 FY budget, the entire ATF agency has 5,100 employees, of whom 3,800 operate in the firearms area, the remaining covering arson, explosives, alcohol and tobacco. Regarding firearms, employees are split about 50-50 between investigations and inspections, with the latter responsible for licensing, tracing and examining records related to gun commerce, while the agents assist other law enforcement agencies in crime investigations involving guns.

Here's how the ATF views itself (from a 2014 fact sheet): "ATF is the U.S. law enforcement agency dedicated to protecting the country from the illegal use of firearms and explosives in violent crime and acts of terrorism. ATF protects public safety by combating firearms trafficking, the improper use and storage of explosives, and the illegal diversion of alcohol and tobacco products." Except there's only one little problem. As I mentioned above, and now I'm going to add a few details, there is no crime known as "gun trafficking," except when someone says something untrue on the 4473 form. Which means that all the talk about "protecting" us from gun crimes consists of looking at the paperwork generated by the movement of guns from one set of hands to another, not actually going after people who commit real crimes.

The ATF might have been able to investigate real crimes had a bill introduced by Congresswoman Carolyn Maloney (D-N.Y.) ever gotten out of the House Judiciary Committee, or even gotten to the full committee, instead of languishing in the Subcommittee on Crime, Terrorism, Homeland Security and Investigations since it was introduced in February, 2013. The bill has 118 co-sponsors, it even has 5 Republican co-sponsors. It's going nowhere. But it's an interesting comment on the law enforcement role of the ATF and here's what it says:

> It shall be unlawful for any person, in or affecting interstate commerce,-- ``(1) to purchase, attempt to purchase, or transfer a firearm, with the intent to deliver the firearm to another person who the transferor knows, or has reasonable cause to believe, is prohibited by Federal or State law from possessing a firearm;
>
> ``(2) in purchasing, attempting to purchase, or transferring a firearm, to

intentionally provide false or misleading material information on a Bureau of Alcohol, Tobacco, Firearms, and Explosives firearms transaction record form; or ``(3) to knowingly direct, promote, or facilitate conduct that violates paragraph (1) or (2).

So here is a "straw sale" by another name, i.e., gun trafficking, and notice that it not only prohibits someone from engaging in a straw sale but also prohibits anyone from promoting a straw sale conducted by someone else. And if you don't think this wouldn't be a serious offense, the penalties include fines, jail sentences of up to 20 years, and additional, consecutive five-year jail terms for anyone who organizes or directs the whole operation even though the actual sale was completed by someone else.

If Maloney's bill had actually become law, the ATF would have been instantly transformed from a bunch of guys sitting around looking at paperwork to a real bunch of law enforcement agents who could go out there and arrest people for real, serious crimes. But without such a statute, the ATF could say that it was protecting us from gun crimes from today to next year, but what its staff was really doing was examining paper forms. And that's not going to lift a law enforcement agency very far off the ground in the law enforcement scheme of things when the competition is the DEA and the FBI. So how do you make yourself important if the law you are sworn to protect doesn't really exist? You act as though it does. Which is how and why *Fast and Furious* came about.

Chapter 3

Abramski v. United States (But it's Really The ATF)

Federal gun law establishes an elaborate system of in-person identification and background checks to ensure that guns are kept out of the hands of felons and other prohibited purchasers. It also imposes record-keeping requirements to assist law enforcement authorities in investigating serious crimes through the tracing of guns to their buyers.

SUPREME COURT OF THE UNITED STATES, ABRAMSKI v. UNITED STATES, CERTIORARI TO THE UNITED STATES COURT OF APPEALS FOR THE FOURTH CIRCUIT.

Last week I decided to buy myself a gun. Why? Because I wanted to. That's why I buy all my guns. Because it's fun to buy a new gun; hold it, play with it, maybe even shoot it. Do I have lots of guns I've never shot? Sure I do. I'll bet I have as many guns I've never shot as my wife has shoes she hasn't worn. That's not fair. She's probably worn them once. So maybe I shot all my guns once. But it doesn't really matter. I'm going to buy it whether I shoot it or not.

So I went on the *Armslist* website and began cruising around various handgun listings for my state. Now if I wanted to buy a rifle I could look at listings not only in my state but any contiguous state because I can lawfully and legally cross the state line into New York, Connecticut or New Hampshire and buy a rifle without registering it when I get back home. But handguns are different. You can only buy a handgun legally in your state of residence if have it shipped back to a dealer, pay him for the transfer, blah, blah, blah, a real pain in the ass. So better to look for a handgun in your own state because that way, unless your state is one of the "bad five" that have made all gun transfers subject to a friggin' 4473, you can take the gun from the guy, give the guy the dough, and as my grandfather used to say, "det's det."

The *Armslist* website is tremendously popular with gunnies as well as anti-gunnies. The gunnies love it because you can buy, sell or barter guns and other equipment and it's more or less cost-free. The anti-gunnies like it because it represents the *deus ex machina* of gun illegality, namely, the fact that anyone can get their hands on a gun, whether they are legally-entitled to own a gun or not, and they don't have to break into someone's house to do it. All they have to do is either find a gun listed by a private seller, or post a listing that they are looking for a particular type of weapon and wait for a response. I know a guy who bought a pretty expensive boat this way, another guy has purchased three or four cars and in one case, driven more than 600 miles round trip to pick one up. But you don't need to fill out a 4473 to buy a car, a lawn-mower or a boat. If you walk into a licensed gun shop and point at this gun or that gun, out comes the goddamn 4473.

So I went browsing through *Armslist* one evening and saw a beautiful Colt 1911 45 Pistol which, according to the description and the engraving on the slide, was what is known as a Series 70 Colt, which were the best commercial Colt pistols ever made. Why? Because the 1970's was just before Colt lost the contract to supply its 1911 model to the Army (actually they were no longer supplying pistols but just replacement parts) and they also had a total monopoly on selling the M-16 rifle both to the American military and allied armed forces God only knows where. So the company stunk of cash, and even though the United Auto Workers got management to sign one exorbitant contract after another, they could afford to pay top dollar to master craftsmen who turned out guns that could only be described as the best of world class.

Just to finish out the story, Colt went from riches to rags so quickly that the glory days were over before anyone even realized they were gone. Not only did Colt lose the pistol contract after a shoddy, double-action 1911 was rejected by the Army in the first round of field tests to replace the handgun carried by soldiers since before World War I, but the M-16 rifle contract began to tail off when armaments funding was cut after Vietnam. It was at this point that the UAW, following nobody's advice but its own, called a strike at the Hartford factory which closed the assembly works down until the company management began hiring non-union replacement employees with little or no skills, and the disappearance of the older, heavily-experienced workforce immediately made itself known with the collapse of quality controls in all the guns.

I had many Colt pistols and revolvers over the years, including a matched set of Diamondback revolvers in 38 and 22, as well as four-inch and six-inch 357 Pythons, with the four-inch probably the most accurate handgun I ever owned. At some point back in the late 80's my Colt collection numbered some forty guns, including a Colt Single Action Army revolver that, according to the letter I received from the Colt history office (for which I gladly paid ten bucks), had been shipped from the Hartford factory to a hardware store in Kansas sometime around 1895. The gun was in pristine shape, including the original grips with the rampant Colt medallions on either side, and while I never shot it for fear of breaking even one of the original springs, the gun cycled perfectly and the cylinder timing was still remarkably strong. I sold the entire collection to some guy who I met at a gun show; he gave me fifteen grand for the entire pile, sight unseen, and the day after he showed up to cart off the stash, I went out and bought myself a beautiful Harley Low Rider which I was hoping would get me some nice-looking chicks when I ran the bike out to the beach. In fact I did get two really pretty young girls who loved being taken here and there on the bike; the problem was that they were my two daughters and within a couple of months I realized I had made a big mistake. So I dumped the Harley and went back to guns.

Over the years since then I've picked up a few Colt handguns now and again, and I couldn't resist the 1911 Series 70 that was listed on *Armslist* last week. The owner, who lived about 40 miles from me, was willing to sell the gun for cash but was also looking for a 9mm pistol in trade, and after the exchange of a few emails we agreed that I would get his Colt and I would give him $350 cash and one of my Glocks—I have a lot of Glocks.

We met the following Sunday morning in front of the Congregational Church on the village green at Ashby, MA. I like doing gun business in front of a church. Gives me that warm and comfortable feeling, like I'm being tended to, if you know what I mean. It took us about five minutes to trade guns, trade gun license numbers and off we went. I handed him the cash in a wad and he didn't bother to count it. What the NRA says is true: gun guys tend to be a law-abiding and honest bunch. At some point over the next couple of days my compatriot in arms contacted me to tell me that he had gone online, registered the sale with the state and, by the way, I had overpaid him by forty bucks.

The way it works in my state—Massachusetts—is like this. If you purchase a gun from a dealer you have to go through the usual 4473 check. If you want to transfer a gun privately you go online and fill out a form which says who gave away the gun, who received it, and the manufacture, type and caliber of the weapon. The person who gives away the gun doesn't need a license, the person receiving it needs a license and the license number is also entered on the online form. In theory, this means that the state but not the feds knows about every gun transfer that takes place. But that's the theory. Here's the practice.

Massachusetts is *not* a registration state. The only legal document you need to prove ownership of every gun in your possession is your gun license, which is issued to you following the same background check at the state level that the feds conduct with the 4473 and is renewable every six years, assuming that you didn't do something like commit a felony which resulted in the license being taken away. So if I decide to get my hands on a gun without going through the state registration process, I am in no way obligated to prove how I got my hands on that gun. Right now I probably own 35 or 40 guns. Give me a week and maybe I'll dig up paperwork on 5 or 6. Not that I bought them "off paper," as we like to say. But since I am not legally obligated to actually hold onto such paperwork, why bother to keep it around?

I think I've bought 5 guns on the *Armlist* website, maybe six. In half the transactions the seller wanted to do all the registration nonsense, in the other transactions he didn't care. I'd be willing to bet you that my experience with legalizing private gun transactions is probably about average—half yes, half no—and if they were to change the law in Massachusetts the way they just changed it in Washington to require a 4473 for all private sales, I'd comply with it and wouldn't very much care. But to be honest with you, my main motivation for going along with universal NICS checks would be the issue of whether or not I thought that in transferring a gun without the required check I might get caught. And I suspect that Bruce Abramski consciously violated the 4473 regulations and consciously involved himself in a straw sale which ended up being reviewed by the Supreme Court because he just didn't think he'd get caught.

Bruce Abramski used to be a cop. He's also a scofflaw. And the reason he's a scofflaw is that in 2009 he walked into a gun shop near where he lives in Virginia and bought a gun knowing that he wasn't buying it for himself. But let's hear it in the words of his attorney who explained what he did to the United States Supreme Court: "He filled out all the required federal paperwork providing his own name and identifying information and passing a background check. He then traveled to his uncle's home in Pennsylvania and delivered the firearm to a licensed gun dealer there. That gun dealer required Mr. Abramski's uncle to fill out the exact same federal paperwork and pass his own background check before taking possession of the firearm."

So how did anyone even find out that Abramski bought the gun for someone else? Because a year later the police showed up at Abramski's house with a search warrant having to do with suspicion that Abramski had helped rob a bank. And while they were nosing around the house looking at this and that, the investigators came across the receipt that Abramski's uncle gave him to prove that he had also mailed him the money which was used to buy the gun. So they asked to see the gun. And they couldn't see the gun because the gun was in Pennsylvania. And that's when the whole deal unraveled and Abramski would ultimately plead guilty to a federal offense, to wit, falsely filling out a 4473.

I love when the Supreme Court decides a case in which the person who is the object of all the legal brouhaha is just some average type or, better yet, something of a lowlife. My favorite legal case of all time is Brown vs. Board of Education because it just so happens that I attended the very first public school that integrated after that momentous decision, West School in Washington, D.C. The city schools which had been segregated had to integrate immediately because the District was federal property, and it was accomplished in two years. The first year was a "pilot" year and my school was chosen to be the pilot; the second year the entire system was integrated. So in a coincidental way, I participated in a moment of real history.

But my second favorite case after Brown is the 1963 Gideon v. Wainwright decision, when the Court decided that everyone was entitled to legal representation in criminal cases under the 14th Amendment. And Gideon was no prize. His crime consisted of allegedly breaking into a crummy little pool hall in Panama City, Florida and jimmying the cigarette machine for the change and some packs of cigarettes. Gideon was a life-long petty thief who was married four times, never had a real job and was in and out of penal institutions, even working himself up to a stint at Leavenworth for stealing federal property. I loved how he was portrayed by Henry Fonda in a movie based on *Gideon's Trumpet* written by Anthony Lewis. But most of all what I loved is that a major landmark case focused on whether the Constitution protected a good-for-nothing like Gideon.

Now I'm not saying that Abramski was anywhere near as bad as Gideon, but neither am I saying that he was the President of the local Kiwanis Club. In fact, had he not been a suspect in a bank robbery case, the cops would never have found the paperwork which showed that Abramski had been involved in a straw purchase of a gun. But what got the whole ball rolling was a little lie that Abramski told the owner of the gun shop where he purchased his uncle's gun, because the shop was offering discounts to active police officers, and while Abramski showed a police ID at the time of the sale, in fact he was not at that time employed as a cop. But his uncle wanted a Glock, and the price was cheaper than what it would have been if his uncle had just walked into a gun shop in Pennsylvania and bought himself a gun.

And here's the real kicker: there would have been no Abramski case and no decision about the constitutionality of the 4473 if Abramski had done what he should have done, namely, gone into the gun store, told the dealer that he was buying the gun for someone in another state, and then let the dealer ship the gun directly to Pennsylvania, where Abramski's uncle would have then gone in, filled out a 4473 and picked up the gun. Except for one little thing; if he had done that he probably wouldn't have gotten the law enforcement discount and his uncle would have had to pay the Pennsylvania dealer a few bucks for processing the 4473 paperwork without making a profit from the actual sale. In other words, the whole 4473 scam took place because Abramski's uncle wanted to save himself a few bucks.

(I need to insert a little point here for which there was absolutely no reference in all of the pleadings connected to the Abramski case. Had Abramski walked in to my shop and given me the gun to transfer to his uncle, I would have told Abramski to take the gun, get back in his car, drive back to Virginia and find a dealer who would ship me the gun. In fact, had I taken the gun from Abramski, as was the case with the dealer in Pennsylvania, I would have been breaking the law established by the GCA68 in the first place, since the whole point of that law was to curb and regulate interstate movement of guns. Abramski could have walked out of the shop in Virginia where he purchased the gun, walked into another Virginia gun shop and asked the latter dealer to ship the gun to the dealer in Pennsylvania and the entire transfer would have been legal, even though Abramski knew that he wasn't buying the gun for himself when he filled out the 4473. Nobody on the Supreme Court or any of the lower courts that heard or read this case ever mentioned this point. So much for how well any of these legal experts understand firearms law.)

The reason I am going into this situation in such detail is because this is what Abramski's lawyer argued before the Supreme Court. After all, he couldn't say that Abramski was buying the gun for himself. His client not only went into the gun shop at the request of his uncle, but even used money that the uncle sent him for the sale. And yet, be that as it may, when Abramski filled out the 4473 he answered the following question, question 11a, by checking the box that said "yes": "Are you the actual transferee/buyer of the firearm(s) listed on this form? **Warning: You are not the actual buyer if you are acquiring the firearm(s) on behalf of another person. If you are not the actual buyer the dealer cannot transfer the firearm(s) to you.** [The form text is bolded.]

So what the question before the Court came down to was this: How does one define the word "buyer" for purposes of understanding the intent and the use of the 4473? Which goes to a much bigger issue, namely, how does one really evaluate the role and activities of the ATF? Because when all is really said and done, the overwhelming rationale for the existence (and cost) of the ATF gets down to investigating who answers question 11a on the 4473, and what do they do with the gun that is the reason why 4473 was filled out in the first place? Or to put it in a more prosaic way, no 4473, no ATF.

Don't make the mistake the way Abramski made the mistake of thinking that the only issue at hand was whether he should have signed the 4473 indicating that he was the "actual buyer" of the gun. Remember, when the Supreme Court agrees to hear a case, it isn't just looking at what happened to Abramski, it's looking at what happened to the law whose substance and purpose needs to be understood in order to figure out whether the law, not the individual who broke it, needs to be clarified, left alone or changed. And the attorney who represented Abramski before the nation's highest court—Richard Dietz—understood this very well. Because when he stood before the bench and made his oral argument, he explained the rationale for the 4473 as: "This legislation, the way Congress designed it, is not focused on sort of the end point. It's not concerned about where a gun is actually going. Who's ultimately going to receive it. What Congress was concerned about was the starting point, because as part of the key political compromise of the Gun Control Act, there were two competing interests that needed to be accommodated."

So now we are back to the origins of the 4473 (and the origins of the present-day ATF), which can only be understood with reference to the GCA68. And what "compromise" is Dietz talking about? This has to do with yet another piece of gun law, known as the Firearms Owners' Protection Act (FOPA) of 1986, which was passed in order to remedy some of the problems that arose in the years after the promulgation of GCA68. There hasn't been much discussion of FOPA over the years, because the pro-gun folks were still willing to accommodate and compromise with the government, a stance they dropped during the debate over the Clinton gun bills in 1993-94, and the anti-gun crowd, who thought they had won a big victory in 1968, now saw some of the provisions of the earlier law either watered down or done away with altogether. To show you how the world has changed, much of the discussion between the two sides over FOPA was facilitated by a gun writer named Dick Metcalf, who was somehow trusted by everyone to keep things on track, but when he came out in 2013 after Sandy Hook and said that there was room for some common-sense gun regulations that would not impair the 2nd Amendment, he was immediately and permanently jettisoned from every pro-gun organization under the sun.

The rationale for FOPA lay in a provision of the GCA68 that was tacked onto the bill just before the final House vote. Known as section 101, it declared that, "it is not the purpose of this title to place any undue or unnecessary Federal restrictions or burdens on law-abiding citizens with respect to the acquisition, possession, or use of firearms." In the years which followed the enactment of GCA68, multiple congressional hearings took place which seemed to indicate that the unnecessary restrictions and burdens being placed on law abiding citizens were coming not from the law itself, but from the way it was being administered by the ATF. In particular, the agency took a very aggressive stance as regards its definition of dealers and used this very narrow definition to harass many gun owners who were doing nothing more dangerous than selling an old gun either to the general public or to a friend.

In one instance, an ATF undercover purchased a 22-caliber target pistol from someone who advertised the pistol and a 22-caliber rifle for sale in a local newspaper in Alexandria, Virginia. The agent returned to the ATF office with the first gun, was instructed to go back and purchase the second gun, whereupon the poor seller was charged with violation of GCA68 because he was engaging in the business of firearms sales without having first applied for, and received, a dealer's FFL. If the ATF had been allowed to expand the scope of its activity to require a dealer's license for the casual sale of some old guns, there would have been an immense of bureaucratic work and investigatory activity that would have required a substantial increase in the size of ATF staff.

Which was actually what the post-GCA68 regulatory world was all about, because shortly after the GCA68 law was passed, there was a remarkable increase in the world price of raw sugar, which propelled an upwards spiral of prices of all food commodities that utilized large amounts of sugar as part of their processing. Remember when a Hershey bar cost ten cents? It went to a quarter in the early 70's and never came back down. The increase in the cost of sugar hit another food industry even harder, except that this food happened to be liquor, in particular liquor made in illegal stills. Between 1972 and 1978, the number of raids on illegal stills dropped from nearly 3,000 to just over 360, which meant that as many as 40% of the ATF field force was sitting around with nothing to do. So GCA68 was a Godsend for the agency, assuming that they could justify agent workloads by dint of ultra-enforcement of gun regulatory laws.

Here's an example of this ultra-enforcement as told to a Senate committee hearing looking into allegations of ATF abuse of GCA68. The individual in question, a disabled war veteran, had set up a little gunsmith business with the help of the VA. The ATF sent an undercover agent onto his premises who tried to entice the smith into partnering in an illegal sale of guns. The gun smith refused, then called the ATF and reported the encounter and went so far as to say that he was willing to testify about the matter in court. What did he get for his trouble? An ATF raid of his premises during which time his entire inventory of guns and gun parts were examined, after which he was charged with possession of a full-automatic weapon for which he did not have a proper NFA license.

In fact it wasn't a whole weapon. It was a lower receiver, the part of the gun which contains the trigger assembly (hence, can fire full-auto if the assembly can operate in that manner) and is stamped with a serial number. The receiver was milled in a way that would have allowed someone to assemble a full-auto weapon, but the smith didn't even know that he was in possession of a Class III (NFA) gun. Like most gun smiths he had gone into business by buying up lots of spare parts for guns from another smith who had gone out of business and this part was lying around along with lots of other junk. Nevertheless, he was charged with a violation, but eventually was cleared by the District Court.

But where the ATF could really flex its regulatory muscles was in their efforts to control the behavior of dealers, for the simple reason that the word "dealer" was not clearly defined in GCA68, and to drum up more business, the ATF took the position, believe it or not, that anyone who sold a gun to anyone else could be considered as dealing in guns. Now in the interests of full disclosure it has to be admitted that the political landscape in Washington and the country in general had changed considerably between the implementation of GCA68 and the congressional hearings in 1979-81 that led up to the passage of the FOPA law in 1984. GCA68 was the handiwork of a Democratic-led Congress and a liberal, albeit Southern liberal President. Ten years later, the political spectrum had shifted Right, the government was getting ready for a guy named Reagan, the congressional committees which heard testimony about ATF abuses were led by Conservative Republicans like Strom Thurmond, and everyone on the red side of the aisle was beginning to cozy up to the NRA.

But at the same time that Republican lawmakers were finding it politically advantageous to assert concerns over protecting 2nd Amendment rights, they also had to be careful to not appear to be lessening the authority of law enforcement agencies, given how well "law and order" themes played back home. So what they did in 1994 was to make a few changes to the way in which the ATF could inspect the records of gun dealers, make the definition of "dealer" slightly more specific so as to distinguish between someone who was really in business as opposed to someone who was just casually or occasionally selling guns, and most of all, to allow the interstate transfer of rifles and shotguns to be conducted without necessitating the intervention of a dealer, thus taking a large chunk of gun traffic activity out of the public (i.e. regulated) sphere altogether.

What the 1994 law did not touch, however, was the authority given to the Treasury Department, and hence to the ATF, to promulgate and therefore enforce the rules that created the regulatory infrastructure in the first place as defined by GCA68.

And this infrastructure, the vast paperwork empire over which the ATF would administer and preside, consisted of information collected by federally licensed dealers to show how guns came into their possession and to whom these guns were then transferred or sold. Because in this way the entire commerce of firearms would move from the private, unseen world to the public and regulated world, thus making it more difficult for guns to end up in the wrong hands. Here's the relevant quote (with my clarification in brackets) from the GCA68 itself: "Upon the request of any State or any political subdivision [law enforcement agencies] thereof, the Secretary [ATF representing the Treasury Department] may make available to such State or political subdivision thereof, any information which he may obtain by reason of the provisions of this chapter with respect to the identification of persons within such State or political subdivision thereof, who have purchased or received firearms or ammunition, together with a description of such firearms or ammunition."

This one sentence buried in the section of GCA68 which describes the legal responsibilities of gun dealers is what gave the ATF its entire regulatory control over guns, a control that has expanded over time to include all kinds of activities that are nowhere mentioned in any language covering ATF authority, ATF responsibility, or ATF anything else. And it was exactly these unauthorized activities, which expanded the ATF's jurisdiction far beyond anything that was statutorily allowable, that the majority decision in Abramski was going to protect. To quote Justice Kagan: "The overarching reason is that Abramski's reading would undermine—indeed, for all important purposes, would virtually repeal—the gun law's core provisions."

And how did Justice Kagan and the SCOTUS majority define the gun law's "core provision?" Not with reference to any law or statute, but to a glossy PR statement put out in 2000 by the ATF in which the agency explained and justified itself and its regulatory activities: *Dept. of Treasury, Bureau of Alcohol, Tobacco & Firearms, Following the Gun: Enforcing Federal Laws Against Firearms Traffickers, (June2000).* I'm going to examine this publication in some detail, but before I get into that discussion it does occur to me that if a court is going to review the legal validity of a petitioner's argument (in this case the petitioner was Abramski), and the argument on questioning the regulatory activities of a particular governmental agency, should the Court be using as its reference for understanding the activities of that agency a PR document put out by the agency itself? Mind you, not that a PR document can't be based on true facts, but I'll let the readers judge for themselves.

The report starts off with a Foreword written by Bradley Buckles, the Director of ATF. Actually, before I even get into his comments, I noticed something interesting about the report's title, i.e., "Enforcing Federal Laws Against Firearms Traffickers," a phrase which is repeated in the fifth sentence of Buckles's commentary when he says, "Historically, the Bureau of Alcohol, Tobacco and Firearms (ATF) has pursued cases against both armed offenders and firearms traffickers." There's only one little problem. There are no federal laws against gun trafficking, the phrase "gun trafficking" or "gun trafficker" doesn't exist in federal law, or federal regulations, or federal anything at all. The ATF, by its own admission, is pursuing "cases" against something that doesn't exist.

In 2013, after Sandy Hook, Representative Carolyn Maloney (D-NY) actually found five Republicans in the House to sign onto something called The Gun Trafficking Prevention Act, which defined a gun trafficker as anyone who "purchased, attempted to purchase with intent to deliver the firearm to another person who the transferor knows or has reasonable cause to believe is prohibited from possessing a firearm; in purchasing, attempting to purchase, or transferring a firearm, from intentionally providing false or misleading material information on a Bureau of Alcohol, Tobacco, Firearms, and Explosives (ATF) firearms transaction record form; or knowingly directing, promoting, facilitating, or conspiring to commit such a violation. Authorizes an enhanced penalty for someone who organizes or supervises such conduct."

It's important to note here that our man Abramski wasn't a gun trafficker. He was a scofflaw. He knew that he was breaking a law by falsely claiming on the 4473 Form that he was purchasing a gun for himself. But the law he was breaking made it a criminal act to knowingly lie on the 4473. It didn't say anything about what he did after he lied and walked out of the gun shop in Virginia with the gun. The fact that Congresswoman Maloney felt impelled to introduce her gun trafficking law (which went nowhere) when all kinds of gun bills were floating around at the Federal and State levels following Sandy Hook is really beside the point. What is the point is that the ATF claimed they were in the business of pursuing firearms traffickers not just since 2000, but "historically" for many years earlier than that.

And whom, exactly, were they pursuing? Anyone they wanted to pursue who, like Abramski, lied on a Form 4473 and thus committed a "straw" sale. Here are some examples of firearms trafficking that the

ATF successfully pursued as divulged in a March, 2013 press release from the United States Attorney's Office in the Eastern District of California:

- Barry Rhodes, 27, was charged with one count of being a felon in possession of a firearm for possessing a 9mm semiautomatic firearm after previously being convicted of a felony.

- A federal grand jury returned a two-count indictment against Stockton resident, Arthurton Warren, 31, charging him with being a felon in possession of a firearm. Court documents allege that he was in possession of a .40 caliber semi–automatic pistol and a sawed–off shotgun after previously being convicted of felony offenses.

- A federal grand jury returned a one–count indictment charging Stockton resident, Hector Montanez, 24, with being a felon in possession of a firearm. Court documents allege that Montanez was in possession of a 9mm Glock pistol after previously being convicted of multiple felony offenses.

- Sacramento Man Indicted for Firearms Trafficking Offenses (2:13–cr–92–GEB); Dejon Andrade, 27, of Sacramento, was indicted today on one count of unlawful dealing in firearms, five counts of interstate travel with intent to unlawfully deal in firearms, and nine counts of illegal transportation of firearms acquired outside of state of residency.

According to court documents, Andrade used a Nevada ID to buy guns in Nevada, although he resided in California. He was prohibited from purchasing or possessing guns in California because of parole conditions, but was able to buy firearms in Reno by providing false information on his federal firearm purchase paperwork (ATF Form 4473). Andrade was found to be in possession of a Sturm, Ruger, Model 95, 9mm pistol, and a Smith and Wesson Model SD40 VE .40–caliber pistol that had been purchased by Andrade in Reno.

These cases were described as indictments for gun trafficking. In fact, the individuals indicted in each case had trafficked guns to themselves. They hadn't sold them to anyone else; they hadn't lied on a Form 4473 to hide the true identity of who was getting the gun; they had answered "yes" to one of the questions which determined whether they fell into one of the legal categories which, under GCA68, made them disqualified from owning a gun. This made them gun traffickers. They did exactly what Bruce Abramski did; they consciously lied on a Form 4473 to get their hands on a gun. Since none of these individuals were charged with selling or giving a gun to anyone else, the fact that they lied on the NICS form means that anyone who walks out of a gun shop after having not been caught saying something that was untrue on the

4473 is not only a scofflaw, but a gun trafficker in the bargain.

But how do you know that someone is a gun trafficker just because they have left a paper trail which, when it is examined during a routine inspection of a gun shop's 4473 collection, shows up with errors on a particular form? Remember our friend Dave LaGuercia of Riverview Sales who sold the AR-15 that Adam Lanza used to mow down those teachers and kids at Sandy Hook? One of the charges against him was that the day he let someone leave the store with a rifle was the day before, not after, he completed the NICS check. Which means that LaGuercia had violated the rules governing 4473. Which meant he was a gun trafficker and so, by the way, was the old man who walked out of the store with the gun. Now if all the ATF could show for its efforts was that somebody didn't correctly fill out a form, nobody would take the agency very seriously. But if you can take those incorrect forms and magically turn them into examples of gun trafficking that you've kept from taking place, then all of a sudden what you do agency-wise becomes much more important. I'm not being sarcastic to prove a point. I'm taking the ATF at their word. Ready? Here's their analysis (in the 2000 trafficking report) of why mistakes on the 4473 need to be understood as a very serious state of affairs:

The most common violation by FFLs associated with trafficking is recordkeeping violations. Failure to keep required records was found in almost half of the trafficking investigations involving FFLs, and the FFL making false entries in the records was found in just under a fifth of these investigations. These violations are primarily misdemeanors, *despite being associated with investigations involving a high volume of trafficked firearms.*[My italics]

"Despite being associated with investigations involving a high volume of trafficked firearms."

Says who? The agency that wants you to believe that when someone makes a mistake filling out a form that this indicates the possibility that the ATF has uncovered a major gun trafficking ring? The fact that a dealer made a "false" entry or didn't catch a customer who made a "false" entry doesn't say anything at all except that something turned up on the 4473 that wasn't true. I know a dealer who purchased virtually all his gun inventory from a single wholesaler and was cited for more than 1,200 errors in his A&D book because he didn't write the wholesaler's federal firearms license number next to the wholesaler's name. This dealer, as far as he knows, was never suspected of being a gun trafficker. But every time he didn't bother to write out the wholesaler's 15-digit license number (as if the ATF didn't know the identity of this national wholesaler who they had inspected around the same time they inspected this dealer), he was, according to the ATF's gun trafficking report, potentially giving the agency grounds for suspecting him of running a gun trafficking operation out his back door.

Here's the problem with trafficking: it was Scalia who nailed it in the oral arguments about Abramski when, in response to the Government's view that a straw sale takes place whenever someone who wants to buy a gun lets someone else buy it for him, he said, "Why is that—why is that any more horrible than the notion that as soon as I buy it I walk out of the store and I meet this guy in the parking lot, he says, 'Hey, that's a nifty looking gun there. How much did you pay for it?' He says, 'You know, I paid 600 dollars.' 'I'll give you 700.' 'Oh, it's yours.' Right? I can hand it to him, can't I?"

What Scalia was getting at was the fact that there was nothing in GCA68 or any other gun law that prohibited a purchaser from turning around, gun in hand, and selling it to someone else either right after he bought it or two years after he bought it. And what if, for example, he walked into a gun shop, saw a gun that he knew was wanted by a friend and bought the gun knowing that he was going to sell it to the friend the moment he saw him? If every such transaction was deemed a "straw" sale, and every straw sale was considered to be a possible instance of gun trafficking, you might be making a lot of work for the agency that was responsible for investigating straw sales, but that agency wasn't necessarily investigating illegal activities at all.

The more I try to figure out the difference between a "legal" and an "illegal" transfer of a firearm between two individuals, the more confused I get. And one of the reasons for all this confusion is that the GCA68 and its successors—FOPA and Brady— start and end the analysis of illegal commerce of firearms by looking only at the initial point of sale, namely, the gun dealer's counter where every gun moves into the civilian market for the first time. And since a certain percentage of guns eventually end up being used in crimes, it has to be assumed that, at some point the gun in question moved from legal to illegal hands. But how do you know when that occurred if gun transfers between individuals, or what the ATF calls "unlicensed dealers," aren't subject to the type of registration that takes place between consumers and federally-licensed dealers every time a gun moves from the dealer's shelf into a customer's hands?

You don't know. So you establish certain criteria that, when met, could indicate that a gun is moving or has moved from the legal to the illegal market by establishing the notion that a good indicator is a "straw" sale. And how do you check to see if a particular dealer's shop may be a location where straw sales take place? By examining his paperwork, his A&D book and his collection of 4473 forms, to see how many mistakes have been made. Because the way the law reads, there is really no difference between someone misstating their legal status on a 4473 because they want to cover up a conviction for a serious crime, and someone accidentally misstating their birthday on the same form which might allow them to pass what otherwise would be a denial when the information is transmitted to NICS. As the ATF says in the Gun Trafficking report, "Straw purchasing itself, that is, the practice of buying firearms from an unlicensed dealer on behalf of someone else, is not unlawful." In other words, you can't lie in a private transaction because there's no paperwork which needs to be filled out. Which brings us back to the primordial role of the ATF, which is to check paperwork.

And not only can paperwork be used to verify whether a particular transaction might or might not be a straw purchase, it can also be used to follow the path of a gun from its initial point of sale all the way through to the point that it is recovered as part of an investigation of a crime. This is known as tracing, and the ATF manages what they refer to as the nation's "only crime gun tracing facility." Let me let you read how the ATF describes what the National Tracing Center does: "The NTC provides critical information that helps domestic and international law enforcement agencies solve firearms crimes, detect firearms trafficking, and track the intrastate, interstate, and international movement of crime guns." The NTC conducted 340,000 such traces in 2013, and all these traces were, according to the ATF, initiated "when a law enforcement agency discovers a firearm at a crime scene and seeks to learn the origin or background of that firearm in order to develop investigative leads."

Think about that. This agency conducted 340,000 traces of guns that were used in crimes, which is a pretty impressive number when you stop and think about it. That's almost 1,000 traces a day. In 2013, according to the FBI, there were roughly 240,000 homicides and assaults committed with guns. Does this mean that the ATF helped law enforcement agencies develop investigate leads in all or most of these cases? Let me break it to you gently. It doesn't mean that at all. In fact, the figure of 340,000 traces, as impressive as it appears, doesn't mean anything. Why? Because the ATF, in trying to bolster its image as a crime-fighting agency, uses the term "crime gun" for every trace when, in fact, what they trace is what law enforcement agencies ask them to trace, whether the gun in question has anything to do with a crime or not.

In order to request the trace of a weapon, the law enforcement agency submits a Form 3312, aka a National Tracing Center Trace Request. On this form is listed all the relevant information about the gun: type, caliber, manufacturer, serial number, owner if known, location where gun was received, and so forth. There is also a space where the requesting agency designates the "crime" with which the weapon is associated, using the criminal coding system developed by the FBI. There are 61 different crime codes from which the requesting agency can pick one or more. The only problem is that many of the codes don't refer to criminal activity, particularly violent criminal activity at all. Code 6199 is tax revenue, 6299 is conservation, 5599 is health-safekeeping, 5999 is election laws, and the trickiest of them all, 0098 is for a "found" gun.

What is a "found" gun? It's a gun that police get their hands on even if it had nothing to do with any particular crime. And how common are such found guns in the overall tracing activity of the ATF? In 2012, this category accounted for 9% of all traced guns. Another category known as "firearm under investigation" accounted for 11% of all traces. Why would a law enforcement agency investigate a gun? For all kinds of reasons. Many of which might or might not have anything to do with an actual crime. Grandpa is carted off to a nursing home, the kids find a bunch of rifles stacked up in a closet and turn them into the local police. And if the cops have nothing better to do that day or, if it is required in their particular jurisdiction, they must make sure that none of the guns were stolen before giving the treasure trove back to the kids.

More than 2,500 traces were conducted on guns in which the "crime" was firing the gun. Where I live if you discharge a weapon within 200 yards of someone else's home you have committed a crime. One day a friend of mine, who happens to be a local police chief, was walking his beloved Jack Terrier along the road near his home. They happened to walk past the home of an elderly man who was sitting on his porch with his own pet dog and the two dogs started barking at each other, the usual sort of thing. All of a sudden, my friend's dog broke his leash and scampered across the old man's lawn, jumped onto the porch and a real exchange of doggie "fuck you, no fuck *you*" began to take place. Whereupon the old man, who wasn't really right in his head, reached inside his front door, yanked out a shotgun and shot my friend's dog good and dead. All they could charge him with was illegal discharge of the gun. And at some point thereafter the charge was dropped but the old man had to give up his gun. And I guarantee you that this gun ended up being traced by the ATF.

In 2012 the ATF traced 13,783 guns involved in homicides, robberies and simple assaults, which constituted slightly less than 6% of the guns traced that year. Now granted, there were other crimes associated with gun traces that were no doubt important and aided law enforcement agencies in their attempts to control crime. Let's not forget to include the 135 traces that were conducted on guns that were picked up during obscenity investigations or the 60 guns that were categorized as being involved in investigations for "vice." Do the cops still have "vice" squads? I haven't heard that word used in forty years. And if the ATF wants to try and justify their existence by telling us that their trace activity is a necessary part of fighting vice crimes, God bless.

I wouldn't find all these numbers so pompously ridiculous if it weren't for the basic fact that there is nothing in GCA68, FOPA or Brady that mentions tracing at all. And here is where we get back to the comment about compromise made by Bruce Abramski's attorney when he stood before the Supreme Court and tried to argue, ultimately without success, that his client had done nothing wrong by lying on the 4473. Because the compromise he was referring to was the decision by Congress to write a law that would, on the one hand, regulate firearm sales as a means of better controlling gun crimes, while at the same time protecting the 2nd Amendment rights of citizens to do what they wanted to do with their own guns.

The reason that Abramski lost at the Supreme Court was because the compromise embodied in GCA68 allowed the government to make sure that when a gun was introduced into lawful commerce for the first time, it did not go either to someone living in a state other than where the dealer was located, or did not get into the hands of a "prohibited" person, namely, a felon, a drug addict, a mental defective or some other category as defined by federal firearms laws. The fact that Abramski believed his uncle was lawfully entitled to purchase a weapon (which it turned out he could) didn't mean that his belief at the time of purchase and the actual status of his uncle were, in fact, both true. He had really no way of knowing, as he was standing in the gun shop in Virginia, whether his uncle was being arrested at the same moment for grand larceny, aggravated assault or worse. And there is nothing in any of the statutes which speaks to the "belief" of the buyer about the legal fitness of anyone to own a gun other than the buyer himself.

And for exactly the same reason, the government's regulation of gun commerce to take place only at the original point of sale, the entire ATF bureaucratic and investigative empire that they have constructed known as the National Tracing Center has no real legal or statutory basis at all. Abramski's big mistake was not that he lied on the 4473, it was that he held onto the receipt from his uncle which showed that he had received the cash before he actually went in and purchased the gun. If the dealer who sold the gun to Abramski had forgotten to fill out his part of the 4473 and then mistakenly put down the wrong date on which he made the NICS call (which was the charge made against LaGuercia), he could also have been charged, like Abramski, with being involved in a straw sale. Note that neither the old man who walked out of Riverside Sales with a rifle or Abramski's uncle to whom his nephew transferred the Glock ever committed or even considered committing a crime with their guns. But the resources of the National Tracing Center were no doubt brought to bear in both cases, resources which, as far as I can tell, operated without reference to any firearm law.

If there was a legal basis for tracing firearms, you have to assume that the ATF would brandish it all over the place. But the best they can come up with is the following statement from a collection of FAQs on tracing that the agency published in 2007:

> "Question: Can you trace a firearm when its possible nexus to a crime is not readily apparent, e.g., a firearm recovered in a sewage drain?"
>
> Answer: Yes. ATF's longstanding position is that investigating the origin of a firearm to develop leads to determine if has been used in a crime constitutes a *bona fide* [ATF italics] law enforcement investigation.

Ever encounter a law called "longstanding position?"

But that's nothing—if you think the ATF has operated without regard to the statutes which brought them into existence, just wait till you see what happens when the ATF goes out and tries to prevent real gun crimes.

CHAPTER 4

THE WACO MESS

In April, 1993, I decided to close my office in New York City and take a trip around the country to who knows where. All I knew is that I wanted to send some time away from New York. I found out that Greyhound was offering a 30-day ticket that allowed you to go anywhere in the United States, from one city to another, and rack up as many miles as you chose for one hundred bucks. I took a bus to Cleveland, then grabbed another bus to Detroit, went out to see my daughter in Ann Arbor, came back to Detroit, over to Chicago, then down to St. Louis, continued west to KC, then Denver and Salt Lake, and eventually the West Coast.

I didn't bother to stay in hotels in each city because I found it easy and comfortable to sleep on the bus. And whenever I got off the Greyhound I would walk around the terminal, sometimes walking quite a distance through a particular town. It didn't matter whether I made it back and got on the same bus; at one point I returned to a terminal, I think it was in Omaha, to see the bus I had been on pulling away from the station and then realized that my duffle with my clothes was still on the rack above my now-empty seat. So I walked across the street to an Army-Navy store, bought another duffle along with some new underpants, t-shirts, a pair of pants or two and some more socks. A toothbrush and a comb I could pick up at the lotions/notions counter in any drug store no matter where I went.

In this unplanned, peripatetic way I managed to work my way all the way across the country and, for the most part, shared my double seat on the bus or a bench in a waiting room either with someone who had recently done jail time or someone who was visiting someone else in jail. After all, if you're a white male wearing denims, carrying a small duffel and riding a Greyhound bus, it's not like you're on your way to an executive training seminar at IBM. So the chances that someone else going to such a seminar will sit down next to you on a Greyhound are slim to none. And if you're a black guy riding a bus, would you have a police record? You'd probably have one even if you weren't riding a bus, and not necessarily through any fault of your own. The bus that I rode out of Detroit was full until it got to its next stop, or I should say stops, which were for the sprawling prison facility in the town of Jackson, and by the time the bus pulled up in front of the last one I was the only person beside the driver who was still on board. Nebraska had two enormous penitentiaries on Interstate 80 at either end of the state. Utah's main prison was a major stop for my bus between Denver and Salt Lake.

I would say without exaggeration that I probably spent the better part of a week with a fairly representative sample of America's felon population, all of whom were either just coming out of jail or waiting to go back in. What I found most interesting about these folks was their basic sense of resignation; they had long gotten over the fact that they had spent substantial amounts of their lives behind bars, and they were all convinced that sooner or later they would be going back for another stretch. None of them talked about how their prison experiences made them want to "go straight." None of them were glad that they had gotten out and now had "another chance." In fact, the one thing they all wanted to talk about was Waco, where the siege of the Branch Davidian compound had ended in a fiery mess the day after I left New York.

The feeling of all the cons I met on Greyhound about Waco was unanimous. Waco was, for them, what they had faced their whole lives—the violence that the government could bring to bear to enforce its codes and laws. Most of these cons had experienced government authority on a petty, first-hand basis; they had been slapped or punched or kicked by cops and guards both within prison and without. That the government could roll up a tank with a flame-thrower at the end of its cannon and incinerate a compound full of men, women and children was simply an extension of the ability of the street-corner cop to enforce the law by taking out a nightstick and whacking someone over the head.

It figures that sooner or later the ATF would want to start doing some head-whacking of its own, stop chasing paper crimes and start bagging real criminals. Which is how the agency ended up creating a tremendous mess at the Branch Davidian compound outside of Waco, an event that not only would become a rallying-cry among the nascent militia movement, but was cited specifically by Timothy McVeigh as one of the chief reasons he sought revenge against the Federal Government by blowing up the Oklahoma City Murrah Federal Building in 1995. The Davidians started out as a fall-off from the Seventh-Day Adventist Church in the 1930's, then established a community outside of Waco which later became known as Mount Carmel, and ultimately morphed into the Branch Davidians led by Vernon Howell who took the name of David Koresh. Like most cults, the group lived a secretive existence, eating and living in common and preparing for Judgment Day, intensively committed to Bible study and strict loyalty to sect leadership. Probably the most famous religious sect of this type had been the Peoples Temple, a Southern California group that migrated to a large agricultural settlement in Guyana where more than 900 residents, including the leader James Jones, died from cyanide poisoning in 1978.

In May, 1992 the McLennan County Sheriff's Department contacted the ATF in Austin with information that the Davidian compound, located in McClennan County, had been receiving large shipments of what appeared to be explosives and firearms. ATF Agent Davy Aguilera was assigned to the case and began investigating Koresh and his followers in early June. Aguilera's investigation would become the basis of the request made by the ATF for a search warrant which, after it was issued, directly led to the February 28 raid on the compound, the deaths of four ATF agents and the 51-day siege that culminated on April 19 with the destruction of the compound and the deaths of Koresh and 75 of his followers.

Aguilera's affidavit deserves to be analyzed in depth, not only because it served as the entire legal basis for the subsequent raid and paramilitary activity that resulted in the deaths of 75 civilians and four law enforcement agents, but because it was an attempt to elevate the status of the agency from chasing paperwork connected to possessing unlawful firearms to capturing individuals whose ownership and use of those guns was going to lead to the commission of serious and violent crimes. It is therefore important to use Aguilera's affidavit not only as an important artifact for understanding the events that led up to the attack and subsequent siege at the Mt. Carmel compound, but also for gaining an insight into the manner in which the ATF viewed its role as a law enforcement agency responsible for enforcement of all federal firearms laws. If, as we shall see, the ATF decided that Aguilera's investigation yielded enough information to conduct a search of the compound for firearms and related components, the acquisition of which constituted possible or actual violations of federal firearms laws, exactly what types of firearms and components might Koresh and his followers have acquired? This is what ATF Agent Aguilera set out to learn when he opened his investigation following communication with the McLennan County Sheriff's office on May, 1992, and in an initial meeting with Lt. Gene Barber of the Sheriff's Department on June 4, 1992.

At this meeting, Agent Aguilera was told that a UPS driver reported to the Sheriff's Department that he had delivered large parcels of what appeared to be munitions and other bomb-making items to the Mt. Carmel compound, and on one occasion when a package accidentally tore open, he saw what appeared to be canisters of black powder and inert grenade casings, the latter often called "pineapples." Aguilera was further told that another shipper had delivered a total of 60 M-16/AR-15 ammunition magazines to the compound, although the Sheriff's Department did not know the name of this shipper and did not know the capacity of these magazines. But based on "my experience and training" (I am quoting directly from the affidavit), Aguilera knew that an AR-15 could be "quickly" converted to full-automatic fire capability "following a relatively simple process accomplished by an individual purchasing certain parts which will quickly transform the rifle to fire fully automatic."

The allegations that Koresh was receiving shipments out of which he could have assembled machine guns and explosive devices was confirmed, according to Aguilera, by interviews with Olympic Arms and Sarco, two gun distributors who had shipped parcels to the Mt. Carmel complex. The shipments from Olympic Arms consisted of 45 upper receivers for AR-15/M16 rifles, and the shipment from Sarco was one M-16 "parts kit," including a sling and magazine. A third interview with another distributor, Nesard Gun Parts, disclosed that they had sold AR-15/M-16 gun parts to Koresh who, by dint of these shipments plus purchases of guns from a local gun shop in Waco, had accumulated more than 100 upper receivers for AR and AK-style rifles, a pile of inert grenade casings, pounds of gunpowder, lower rifle receivers, and thousands of 9mm and 223 ammunition rounds, adding up to expenditures in excess of $44,000. Quite an arsenal, right?

Aguilera also interviewed Robert Cervenka, who farmed property adjacent to the Mt. Carmel location and reported hearing automatic gun-fire from the compound at the beginning of 1992. The witness stated that he was "familiar" with the sound of automatic fire because he had served overseas with the Army, and therefore was convinced that what he heard was 50-caliber machine guns and "possibly" M-16 automatic fire. It should be noted, incidentally, that a 50-caliber machine gun is quite unlike an M-16 rifle, the latter being a relatively light, hand-held weapon, the former being a large, tripod-mounted piece of equipment often used on heavy military vehicles like tanks and Humvees. One does not just "assemble" a 50-caliber machine gun with a few store-bought parts. And while none of the shipments sent to Koresh contained any parts that could have been used for building a 50-caliber machine gun, Aguilera now had what he believed to be credible testimony that the Branch Davidians had acquired such a weapon and had practiced using it.

There was only one little problem with Agent Aguilera's investigation. At no point was he able to determine whether, in fact, Koresh had actually violated any federal firearms laws, notwithstanding his evident interest in amassing a fairly large collection of guns, ammunition and assorted other firearms crap.

For example, the AR-15/M-16 rifle consists of two sections, which are known as upper and lower receivers. The upper receiver holds the bolt and hammer mechanisms, and is attached to the barrel. The lower receiver holds the trigger assembly and the parts connecting the trigger to the hammer, which in popular jargon is usually referred to as the gun's "action," but also in more technical terms consists of several parts of which the most important is a small metal connecting rod known as the "sear."

Now what the sear does is either allows the hammer to fall repeatedly on the bolt and firing pin, using only the gun's recoil (and the force of the gas that escapes when the shell explodes) to fire subsequent rounds, or it locks the hammer which can then only be released to fire the subsequent round if and when the trigger is again pulled. The former makes the weapon an automatic gun, the latter makes it semi-automatic. The sear is the one part that must be changed in order to convert a semi-automatic gun into full-automatic mode (or vice-versa), and this part, when transferred, constitutes a National Firearms Act transfer requiring the same registration, paperwork and purchase of a Treasury tax stamp which occurs every time someone purchases a fully-assembled auto-fire gun. Can someone cut and polish such a part using a lathe and other metal-fabrication machinery? Of course. Could someone go on the internet and find instructions for how to cut and shape a full-auto sear to turn an AR-15 into an M-16? Is there anything you can't find on the internet?

Agent Aguilera never found any paperwork or other evidence which indicated that Koresh purchased or otherwise acquired any full-auto sears. He also could not find any evidence that the Branch Davidians had ever purchased any fully-automatic weapons, and certainly not a 50-caliber machine gun. It did appear to be the case that the compound contained at least one 50-caliber sniper rifle, but those are bolt-action guns that can accurately fire a 50-caliber shell over distances of a half-mile or more, and the only connection such weapons bear to a 50-caliber machine gun is that they use the same caliber shell.

It's important to point out, incidentally, that Aguilera and the ATF made no attempt to obscure or hide their investigative activity from the subject of all this effort, namely, Vernon Dean Howell aka David Koresh. How did Koresh learn about the investigation? Because Aguilera spoke with him on the phone the day he visited a local gun dealer, Henry McMahon, who had been telling customers about all the guns he was selling to the Mt. Carmel compound which, when Aguilera checked McMahon's books, totaled roughly 35 guns. The visit to McMahon's shop, which was actually located in his home and was represented by Aguilera and another agent as just a routine examination of his records, also turned up the absence of 65 AR-15 lower receivers which, according to McMahon, were being stored for him at the home of Koresh. A brief discussion ensued about how this arrangement technically was a violation of ATF regulations, whereupon McMahon telephoned Koresh who then spoke to Aguilera and invited the ATF agent to come by the compound immediately to view the guns.

At this juncture the ATF had been investigating the possibility of weapons violations by the Branch Davidians for nearly two months. They had interviewed members of the McLennan County Sheriff's Department, officers from the Texas

Rangers, neighbors and other locals, employees of at least four mail-order firearms distributors, and had engaged the services of additional ATF munitions and firearms experts in California and Washington, DC. The ATF was now listing this investigation as "sensitive," thus coming under the purview of senior management in the Houston office, and was conducting its efforts in coordination with Bill Johnston, an Assistant U.S. Attorney in Waco. In other words, a lot of time and effort had been expended on an investigation which, to date, had not yielded a single scrap of actual evidence that Koresh and his followers had done anything wrong. Nobody had been in the compound, nobody had interviewed Koresh, all that had been going on was a lot of second-hand evidence collecting, much of it based on nothing more than rumor, innuendo or both. Wouldn't you think it would have been worthwhile for the agent running this effort to at least have a face-to-face meeting with Koresh in order to get some idea of the type of individual who was at the center of all this work? After all, it wasn't as if the investigation could be kept secret any longer since Aguilera was talking by phone to Koresh about weapons that were allegedly stored at the Mt. Carmel compound, right? Koresh had to know at this point that his acquisition of weapons and ammunition was now of interest to the ATF, right?

So what did Aguilera do when Koresh invited him to visit the compound, a visit that Koresh said could happen the same day? Aguilera turned down the invitation! I find it interesting that this telephone conversation between Aguilera and Koresh was nowhere mentioned in the affidavit that Aguilera submitted to the federal magistrate in support of the search warrant that was issued on February 25, 1993. But this omission should not surprise, because the whole tone of the affidavit was to create an atmosphere of secrecy and alleged misdoings at the compound that would reinforce the notion that Koresh and his followers were stockpiling all those weapons and explosives in order to plan and execute something really destructive, really sinister and really big. And this aura of secrecy and furtive planning for some kind of highly destructive event was right in keeping with popular prejudices about Armageddon-prophesying cults like the Branch Davidians whom, it was assumed, would carry out some massive attack to announce that Judgment Day had finally arrived.

I can understand why Aguilera may have been following appropriate investigative techniques by rejecting Koresh's invitation to visit the Mt. Carmel redoubt when he inspected Henry McMahon's shop on July 30. Perhaps he wasn't prepared for such a confrontation and needed time to develop an appropriate set of questions as well as a list of material goods that he might ask to see. Or maybe it would have been risky for him to enter the compound without a security plan to protect himself from assault and without security backup available in case he felt threatened while he was inside the compound's gates. All of these are valid explanations for why Aguilera would turn down an unanticipated invitation from his main quarry whom he had now been pursuing for the better part of two months. And these explanations didn't come off the top of my head; they were proffered by several seasoned law enforcement agents with whom I have shared the contents of this chapter, as well as the sources on which this chapter is based.

Nevertheless, there was a middle ground that Aguilera could have followed between either showing up at the compound after finishing with McMahon, or rejecting Koresh's invitation which is what he did; namely, Aguilera could and should have suggested that he would re-make contact with Koresh, keep him "warm," so to speak, and attempt to gain entrance at a later date when contingency plans could have been developed and put in place. Which is exactly what Aguilera did not do. He did not, at any time, attempt to make further contact with Koresh, and as I will shortly discuss, the undercover agents that the ATF infiltrated into the compound just before the actual assault took place was a classic case of much too little, much too late.

Instead of attempting to open a direct line of communication with Koresh and other members of the Branch Davidian sect holed up at the Mt. Carmel compound, agent Aguilera chose instead to fill up his case dossier by interviewing the most unreliable witnesses of all; i.e., former sect members who had broken with Koresh, bailed out of the sect, physically removed themselves from Mt. Carmel and Waco, and had every reason to want to paint as negative a picture as possible of the situation they had left behind. And even more damaging to the credibility of this investigation, nowhere in any of the statements made by Aguilera or anyone else in the ATF is there the recognition that anyone took the trouble to learn anything about why people join religious cults, how their behavior may then be modified as a result of the cult's lifestyle, and whether anything former cult members say after leaving a cult can be trusted until and unless they have been deprogrammed or analyzed by someone with expertise and experience in the psychology of cult membership. This is particularly important in the Waco situation, because it is important to bear in mind that until the first shots were fired when the ATF attempted to raid the compound on February 28, there was absolutely no evidence which showed that the Branch Davidians, either as individuals or as a group, had ever engaged in any kind of criminal behavior at all.

The one time the cult was investigated took place in February, 1992, when the compound was visited by Joyce Sparks, of the Texas Department of Human Services who, along with several other HS employees and several Sheriff's Deputies, went to Mt. Carmel in response to a complaint from another state alleging that Koresh was operating a "commune-type" compound and was sexually abusing young girls. She was escorted through part of the building, observed nothing particularly significant, then returned in April at which time she was escorted through parts of the compound by Koresh himself who showed her, among other areas, an indoor shooting range, as well as an area in which guns were locked away so that they could not be used by children living in the compound. During this visit, Koresh made idle talk about being a "messenger" from God, about the world coming to an end, about how God would "reveal" himself and lead a military-style operation against the "non-believers" in Waco. Although Aguilera put enough stock in this testimony to include it in his affidavit seeking a search warrant for Mt. Carmel, to the credit of Joyce Sparks and the Texas Department of Human Services, no charges against Koresh were filed and no reason could be found to extend the investigation any further.

Given the fact that the Branch Davidians had never behaved in a manner that might have been a threat to the Waco community, the only rationale for interviewing former cult members would be to determine whether, in fact, the behavior within the compound might have been construed as a threat to members of the cult themselves. But remember that such an investigation would have been far beyond the responsibility or charter of the ATF, whose sole purpose was to determine whether guns and explosives had been acquired illegally or, if they had been acquired legally, whether they were going to be used in the commission of crimes. And since there was no evidence at all of any illegal acquisition of weapons, agent Aguilera then began constructing a never-never land of possibilities, conjectures, hypotheses and other vague investigative wanderings based on testimony of individuals whose ability to tell the truth was suspect by dint of their former Davidian membership, and whose testimony was never validated or verified by any reliable source.

Let's take a look at the testimony of the Bunds family, for example. Chief among this group was Jeannine, who left the Davidians in 1991. According to her, Koresh had exclusive sexual access to all women, married or single, who lived in the compound, although it was not clear whether he ever had sexual relations with Jeannine Bunds herself. According to Jeannine's daughter, Robyn, there was a sexual relationship between herself and Koresh which resulted in the birth of a son. David Bunds was never interviewed, but his wife, Deborah, had been a member of the Davidians since birth. All three women were interviewed by Aguilera in December, 1992 and January 1993. They all identified AK-47s from pictures shown to them by Aguilera and all three said they had witnessed Koresh firing these weapons and others, both in semi-automatic and full-auto mode. Along with daily shooting practice, Koresh also evidently had daily sexual practice, since the senior Mrs. Bunds stated that he had fathered "at least" fifteen children from women in the compound, including several girls who were twelve years old.

During January, 1993 Aguilera also found time to interview Marc Breault who lived at the Mt. Carmel compound from early 1988 until September 1989. While at the compound Breault participated in shooting sessions and also stood armed guard with a loaded weapon which, if necessary, he could use to "shoot to kill" anyone who attempted to gain entrance to the compound. The interview with Breault was also included in the search warrant affidavit by Aguilera, who somehow neglected to mention the fact that Marc Breault, at the time he lived at Mt. Carmel, happened to be legally blind. This would have made for a very interesting situation had Breault, in fact, ever taken upon himself to "shoot to kill."

The most damaging testimony presented by Aguilera to the Federal Magistrate in the application for the search warrant came from a former Davidian member, David Block, who lived at the compound for three months in mid-1992. Block claimed to have seen metal lathes and milling machines of the type that could be used for fabricating and manufacturing gun parts, although he never saw an actual gun part being made. He also stated that the he had seen several "clandestine" gun publications, including Shotgun News, a comment designed to raise more suspicions about whether Koresh and other Davidians were, in fact, engaged in illegal or illicit arms production. Shotgun News is so clandestine that I used it to advertise guns that I was importing in 1995 because its "clandestine" circulation at that time was well over 400,000 copies and it was published three times per month.

Block's testimony is important because he was the only individual interviewed or quoted by Aguilera who claimed to have actually seen what could have been a workshop for converting legal, semi-automatic weapons into illegal, full-auto guns. And had Koresh wanted to build an arsenal of automatic weapons he would have had no choice but to convert semi-auto guns, because in all of the purchases of guns, parts, equipment and crap that the Davidians received, there was not a single automatic weapon, nor were there any automatic sears that could have been used to convert the guns without going to the trouble of milling and fabricating parts.

Following the abortive raid and siege, the government produced piles of paperwork to justify its decisions to investigate Koresh for weapons violations. This paperwork included two reports commissioned by the Treasury Department and prepared by a company called Tioga Engineering, which was owned by William Davis, formerly a ballistics engineer employed by the federal government in a variety of roles involving development and testing of small-arms ammunition and components. The two reports, in the form of letters written from Tioga to a Treasury Department official, were requested to cover whether the ATF had probable cause for seeking a search warrant of the Mt. Carmel campus based on the suspicion that Koresh and others had violated federal firearms laws. And what laws were of particular concern? Laws covering the manufacture, assembly and/or ownership of automatic weapons.

Both reports conclude that based on the shipments received by Koresh in 1992, the Davidians were preparing for some kind of confrontation. They further conclude that the large cache of rifles acquired by Koresh were capable of being converted into fully-automatic weapons, except that Koresh had not received a single automatic sear. In fact, Koresh had not received any item that was illegal or unlawful for him to own. In other words, prior to February 28, there was no evidence that Koresh or his followers had broken any federal firearms laws at all. Therefore, the fact that the Davidians were buying large numbers of guns was not, in and of itself, particularly in a state like Texas, a reasonable cause to conduct a search. What would have to be shown or at least demonstrated by the evidence uncovered by Aguilera was an intent to commit federal gun crimes by converting these legally-purchased weapons and parts into illegal, fully-automatic guns. And how was this intent demonstrated to the satisfaction of the experts from Tioga Engineering, who ultimately agreed that the ATF should not be blamed for going ahead with their tactical plans? Because of the existence of machinery that could be used to fabricate auto sears in lieu of illegally acquiring such sears from somewhere else. Note the comment from the Tioga report of August 3:

> Given one specimen as a pattern, a skilled machinist, having access to a milling machine with appropriate tooling, could produce serviceable "drop-in" automatic sears.

Note the comment from the Tioga report of August 5:

> The material made available does not indicate that the Branch Davidians received shipments containing automatic sears. However, with the machine tools known to exist within the compound, a knowledgeable and motivated individual could easily modify AR-15 lower receivers for installation of military-type automatic sears, or fabricate automatic sears of the drop-in style.

And how did the ballistics experts who wrote these two reports know of the existence of milling machinery in the Mt. Carmel compound? Because Agent Aguilera told them that this equipment was in the compound. Did Agent Aguilera see this machinery when he visited the compound? He never visited the compound. Did Joyce Sparks from the Texas Department of Human Services see this equipment when she visited the compound? No. Did the ATF undercover agent who got into the compound shortly before the assault was initiated see such equipment? No. In fact, the one person who allegedly saw this equipment was none other than David Block, who stayed at the compound for several months in 1993.

Who was this one individual whose testimony was so important in influencing the view that Koresh and his followers were preparing a violent and therefore serious action that required a para-military invasion of the Mr. Carmel campus by the ATF? He was a former Mt. Carmel resident who, shortly after quitting the compound, met up with a professional cult de-programmer named Rick Ross, who earned a living by aggressively chasing after former cult members and using information extracted from these individuals to bolster his own credentials and thus serve as a consultant to organizations that wanted to learn more about a particular cult. At one point he was hired as a consultant about the Davidians both by the ATF and the FBI, the latter wanting some advice on how to negotiate with Koresh during the siege. But the bottom line is that both he and Block had every reason, remunerative above all, to paint the Davidians in a way that would motivate law enforcement to upgrade their perception of a threat, and the testimony by Block and Ross were the only statements made by anyone alleging that Koresh possessed the machinery to create a full-auto arsenal out of the legal, semi-automatic rifles that he had acquired over the previous years.

I am not suggesting that the Branch Davidians posed no threat to the surrounding community, insofar as the compound was located less than four miles from heavily-populated neighborhoods in Waco. I am also not suggesting that the speedy acquisition of more than 100 assault-style rifles along with additional rifle-making receivers and parts shouldn't have been grounds for serious concerns on the part of a government agency which was mandated to regulate traffic in small-arms and look for the possible use of these arms in criminal affairs. What I am questioning in this chapter is the fact that the ATF not only took it upon itself to conduct the investigation into possible violations of federal firearms laws, but then catapulted this activity into something much larger; i.e., a para-military exercise to serve a warrant for a search that might have yielded answers to whether or not any laws had been broken at all. And it is clear that the ATF made a unilateral decision to engage in a large-scale tactical exercise because other, less spectacular options were simply ruled out.

To begin, there was the refusal of Agent Aguilera to meet with Koresh at the compound or even to attempt to maintain contact with him after the initial invitation was refused. The rationale for the ATF's decision to plan and execute a major military-like operation based on the alleged difficulty in contacting Koresh was simply not true. In addition to his willingness to host Aguilera at the compound, he had allowed the Texas Human Services employee access to the property on two occasions, and then showed up at her office in Waco, albeit on the wrong day, to continue the interview with her before she closed the case.

As far as I can tell, there was also no discussion at ATF about whether there was any reason to do anything at all. The agency had placed several operatives in a secure location adjacent to the Mt. Carmel property, and they were able to monitor comings and goings at all hours of the day and night. The ATF could also intercept and inspect any shipment that were received by the Davidians, as well as tap phones, check mail and, most of all, observe any suspicious activity or sudden movements of people or vehicles in and around the site. Finally, since Koresh had shown little resistance to the appearance and access of social services staff, why couldn't the ATF get staff from other government agencies to attempt visits and make observations about what they saw inside the compound if and when they got past the front gate? It turned out, incidentally, that the Davidians were using some of the pineapple grenade containers for decorative items in which they would cut the grenade cover in half, attach it to a piece of wood, lacquer the whole thing and sell it as a cutesy furnishing at local craft and gun shows. Could there have been a chance that they were thinking of building AR-15s with all those kits, using parts to customize fully-made rifles and selling both at gun shows? They didn't need a federal firearms license to do any of those activities in Texas, and for all anyone knows, an AR-15 assembled by a devout Christian sect might have gone over well as a conversation piece.

What I found most remarkable about the argument proffered as to the extreme danger represented by Koresh was the statement in the affidavit developed by Aguilera and repeated in the official Treasury report that the ATF undercover operative, Robert Rodriguez, had seen a videotape in the compound produced by the Gun Owners of America that "portrayed ATF as an agency who violated the rights of gun owners by threats and lies." Is Aguilera serious? Would a federal agency put such crap in a legal document that it was using to justify not only a search warrant but an armed assault on the site where the search warrant would be served? I have some news for the ATF and the Treasury Department, which is that they would hear the same views expressed, or worse, if they walked into any gun shop in the United States, assuming of course, that nobody knew that they represented the ATF. If their identity were known, the comments would probably be nastier and certainly contain a lot more profanity.

The investigations that were conducted by the Executive branch and by Congress after Waco focused primarily on what led up to the end of the siege and the extreme loss of life that took place when a huge fireball erupted and almost the entire compound burst into flames on April 19. To the extent that the ATF's initial investigation was reviewed, both investigations only went so far as to acknowledge that "probable cause" existed for the issuance of a search warrant, whereas the manner in which that investigation relied on terribly-flawed information was largely overlooked. Agent Aguilera and his ATF colleagues had every reason to believe that the acquisition of an arsenal of military-style weapons represented a potential threat, and they also had good reason to suspect that if Koresh and his followers wanted to convert their semi-auto rifles into full-auto weapons, that such an activity could have been accomplished with resources that, if not on the Mt. Carmel campus, could be easily acquired and used.

The problem with the ATF approach, however, is that the agency based its entire investigation on an assumption that this was the only explanation for the Davidian's interest in acquiring so many arms. And there is nothing in the record that speaks to the possibility that any other reason for the cult's behavior was ever considered at all, let alone coming up with alternative scenarios that should have been played out. This pre-determined mind-set that Koresh had one goal and one goal only, namely, to create an arsenal that could be used in the furtherance of a plan to wipe out half of Waco or God knows where else, flows through all the documentation associated with the investigation. Note the conclusion from the August 3 report written by a ballistics engineer who was relying on the documentation assembled by the ATF investigative team:

> It is my conclusion that the quantities and types of military and/or paramilitary items purchased by Koresh and his followers between February 1992 and December 1992 indicate that he was preparing for what he perceived would be all-out armed conflict against the forces of civil authority.

There is simply nothing of any substantive value in the reports of investigations by the ATF which substantiates the statement made by William Davis quoted above. To believe such a statement and discard any alternate explanation or possible alternate explanation is to have created a mind-set in which the possibility of the violation of firearms laws would lead to drastic and overwhelmingly violent results. By the time Aguilera finished his initial interviews and did his initial analysis of shipping invoices and the like, the ATF had already decided that this case had gone far beyond a simple case of violating gun laws. Koresh was clearly involved in a very serious conspiracy to commit very serious crimes, and the ATF was going to demonstrate that it could develop and implement a response.

And what was the threat to which the ATF was responding? The threat, repeated again and again throughout every narrative employed by the ATF to justify their behavior, was the threat posed by the possible existence of automatic weapons. To put it bluntly, the ATF had machine guns on their collective brains. And the reason for this tunnel-vision approach to the problem was that only the threat posed by the possibility of machine gun ownership would really justify the degree of response made by the ATF on February 28, 1993. Nobody in the higher reaches of the ATF would have ever approved a military-style raid on the Mt. Carmel compound if all the compound would have yielded would have been a bunch of completely legal, semi-automatic guns. The ATF, who was after all America's agency responsible for knowing about guns, could certainly be trusted at the field level to create and file reports which adequately assessed the possibility that automatic weapons might be found. Except the reports they filed said nothing of the sort. The reports simply demonstrated how little the agency actually knew about the firearms whose commerce and use it was supposed to regulate and oversee.

CHAPTER 5

ANOTHER MESS: FAST AND FURIOUS

We found that what began as an important and promising investigation of serious firearms trafficking along the Southwest Border that was developed through the efforts of a short-staffed ATF enforcement group quickly grew into an investigation that lacked realistic objectives, did not have appropriate supervision within ATF or the U.S. Attorney's Office, and failed to adequately assess the public safety consequences of not stopping or controlling the alarming purchasing activity that persisted as the investigation progressed.

A Review of ATF's Fast And Furious Operation And Related Matters. Office of the Inspector General, Department of Justice, P. 209.

What saved the ATF's hide after Waco was the even greater bungling of the FBI who ended the siege on April 19 by burning the Mt. Carmel compound to the ground. And even though the ATF brass was subsequently dragged before this investigative committee and that investigative committee, public attention continued to be riveted on the fireball that exploded inside the building, immolating 76 people, against which the death of five ATF agents and six Davidians on February 28 seemed like old hat. The fact that the Clinton Administration had just begun operations in Washington and the Attorney General, Janet Reno, had not yet been confirmed when the raid commenced made it difficult for anyone on the Republican side of the aisle to challenge the exculpatory Democratic-led investigations which followed and basically let the ATF off the hook.

The Agency would not be quite as lucky when details of the *Fast and Furious* operation began to be known. This time the problem surfaced when a U.S. Border Patrol agent, Brian Terry, was shot and killed in a December, 2010 firefight near the Arizona-Mexico border when he and a fellow agent attempted to stop a vehicle carrying what they believed were illegals coming into the U.S. It's not clear exactly which weapon fired the bullet that killed Terry, but one of the guns that was seized after the incident was an AK-47 that had been purchased in a straw sale believed to have been sanctioned by the ATF. And where did this "belief" first appear? On the internet, where else. And who first began circulating stories about the ATF's apparent willingness to sanction straw sales of semi-automatic assault rifles? Several ATF investigators who had expressed their concerns about this activity to agency higher-ups and had evidently been told to stick their concerns you-know-where.

In fact the use of straw sales to trace the movement of illegal guns between the U.S. and Mexico had been going on since at least 2006, when the ATF set up a gun dealer in Arizona with a video recording device that could be used to film straw sales. The operation began with the purchase of 20 lower AR receivers at a gun show in March, 2006, a sale that was reported by the dealer to the ATF because the buyer, in addition to being only 18 years old, paid in cash and asked if he could purchase an additional 50 receivers when they became available. This and later purchases were allowed to go forward without ATF intervention because the agency believed and hoped that the young buyer would lead them to the location where these lower receivers were being assembled into complete firearms and therefore expose the workings of a major gun-trafficking operation.

Not only was the ATF unable to follow the purchaser to what they referred to as a "machine gun conversion shop," but they were unable to track him to any particular location because after exchanging the guns for the money, the buyer simply drove off and quickly distanced himself from the vehicle that was supposed to follow him to see where he would go. The next time the suspected gun-runner showed up it was to tell the dealer that he couldn't make good on his next purchase because he didn't have the money, but the whole caper was rescued by yet another purchaser who showed up and produced the necessary cash. Again, the second buyer drove off with the guns and quickly disappeared.

So now we had at least two instances of what were considered straw sales involving large numbers of assault weapons, or at least the serialized lower receivers that could be assembled into complete firearms, but nobody had seen these straw purchasers actually attempt to transfer or sell the guns to anyone else. Now, it's pretty hard to imagine that someone would have a need to purchase and then retain 75 assault rifle receivers for their personal use. But let's track back for a minute to the Waco investigation because, believe it or not, what got the ATF interested in Koresh in the first place was a report that he had purchased a bunch of lower receivers from a dealer in Waco which the ATF believed he was going to assemble as automatic weapons for use when Armageddon Day finally arrived.

But the purchase of those 35 receivers by Koresh was not a violation of any law. And if he had assembled the receivers into semi-automatic weapons, then kept them in the compound so that other Davidians could shoot them, this also did not contravene any laws. Actually, what appears to be the case is that Koresh was planning to assemble AR-15s out of legally-purchased parts, find a dealer who would sell the perfectly-legal guns at a gun show, then split the profits with neither party having engaged in any illegal activity at all. And the fact that in 2006 a kid named Gonzalez walked away from a dealer in Tucson carrying 20 lower AR receivers was, in and of itself, no less legal than Koresh taking 35 AR receivers from Henry McMahon's gun shop in 1992 and driving back to the compound at Mt. Carmel.

Even without a warrant or any indication that Gonzalez was going to do something illegal with the lower receivers he had purchased, the ATF could have conducted a "knock and talk" visit to his home to see whether he would be willing to talk about why he had purchased the guns. They didn't need probable cause to conduct such a visit, and the worst that would have happened is that Gonzalez would have refused to discuss the matter, but then he would have known that any further purchasing activity would probably be scrutinized both by the ATF and local law enforcement. Which at this point would have probably ended the ATF's interest in Gonzalez, which would have meant that another gun trafficking investigation was going to remain the way that most such investigations remained: an event that would hardly mark the ATF as a front-line law enforcement agency protecting America from the public threat posed by illegal guns.

So the decision was made to let Gonzalez walk away with his first batch of receivers, and get the dealer to encourage Gonzalez to make more transactions in the hopes that he would lead them to bigger and better suspects who, in turn, could ultimately provide the ATF with enough information to bust up a major gun-running ring that stretched between Mexico and the United States. In other words, figure out how to turn one possibly illegal transaction into a big deal. Which is exactly what the ATF tried to do in an operation that was called Wide Receiver but, in fact, bore a much greater resemblance to the Keystone Cops.

Over the next fourteen months the ATF allowed seven different suspects to purchase at least 474 weapons which they believed were all resold as is to drug cartel members or were first converted into full-automatic weapons and then sold to drug cartel members. Very few of these guns were ever recovered except after they were picked up at crime scenes and had thus probably been used in the commission of crimes, no machine shop where guns might have been converted or assembled was ever found, no major gun trafficker big shot was ever indicted or even identified, ATF agents consistently lost track of vehicles they were following which contained straw-sale guns (the consistency of the ATF's inability to maintain moving surveillance on suspects was remarkable), and on several occasions when the ATF mounted GPS devices on individual weapons to pinpoint the location of the guns, the devices quickly failed.

The ATF did gain some valuable experience in utilizing gun dealers to act as informants, despite the fact that they were aware of but ignored the possible conflict that existed because the same agency that was using a dealer as an informant in a criminal matter was also responsible for regulating and monitoring the dealer's activity and compliance with federal gun laws. So while one branch of the ATF conspired with the dealer to violate federal gun laws in furtherance of a criminal investigation, another branch was investigating and warning this same dealer that he was liable for infractions of the federal gun codes. At one point the dealer's books were inspected, infractions unrelated to *Wide Receiver* were identified, and he was ordered to appear at a hearing to decide whether he would be able to retain his license which, if it had been withdrawn, would have quickly terminated his role in the *Wide Receiver* affair.

Operation *Wide Receiver* was wound down at about the same time that Michael Mukasey became the last Attorney General to serve under George Bush, being approved by the Senate on November 16, 2007. One week after he took office, he was prepped for a meeting with high-level law enforcement officials from Mexico to discuss cross-border smuggling of people, drugs and guns. According to Mukasey, he was never told about Operation *Wide Receiver* at this meeting, nor was he informed that ATF agents from the Tucson office had attempted without any real success to coordinate Operation Wide Receiver with law enforcement counterparts in Mexico. And even though such contacts would have required all sorts of notifications to branches of the Justice Department that dealt with foreign law enforcement activities, evidently nobody involved with Wide Receiver believed this to be necessary.

Since Mukasey could not and did not provide any memo that he was given by the ATF or others in preparation for this meeting, we will never know whether or not he knew about Operation *Wide Receiver*. But what we do know is that when he was interviewed by the OIG as part of the Justice Department's investigation of *Fast and Furious* (the report of which has formed the basis for parts of this chapter), he was actually somewhat confused about whether the ATF allowed straw-bought guns to leave locations where they were purchased without interdiction, or whether the ATF allowed contraband materials to be received by dealers without interdiction. In other words, who knows what was known and what wasn't known? Nobody.

You would think that a government agency which expended so much time and resources on an operation that not only yielded such small results but jeopardized public safety would go back, review procedures from top to bottom and make necessary changes either to personnel, procedures or both. You would think that a federal law enforcement agency whose senior management either lied to the Attorney General of the United States or forced the Attorney General to lie would, if nothing else, ensure that no such operation that resulted in such a mess be mounted again. You would think that the ATF would do something either to fix what went wrong or at least acknowledge that things needed to be fixed. Know what the ATF did? They took what they had done in *Wide Receiver*, expanded the number of cooperating dealers, increased the number of straw sales by five-fold, utilized even more agency resources to manage what they were doing and remounted the entire program under a new code name: *Fast and Furious*. As a result, not only did the ATF commit all the same mistakes in *Fast and Furious* that they committed in *Wide Receiver*, but the threat to public safety that had been an issue from the beginning of *Wide Receiver* became a tragic reality when a border patrol agent, Brian Terry, was mowed down in a gunfight in which the arsenal belonging to the bad guys included a weapon that had been walked out of a gun shop by the ATF.

As opposed to *Wide Receiver*, which was run out of the Tucson office of the ATF, *Fast and Furious* was a product of the Phoenix ATF operation, but it began in exactly the same way, namely a message from a federally licensed gun dealer that he believed he had sold some guns to a gun trafficker on October 31, 2009. In fact it turned out that this particular dealer had been notifying the ATF about suspicious gun purchases in his shop from as early as 2001, but this was the first time that such a transaction apparently provoked some interest on the part of the Phoenix ATF staff. In other words, *this dealer had been telling the ATF for eight years that he was concerned about the identity and behavior of some of his customers.*

Over the next month, ATF agents identified five individuals who were evidently making large purchases from several dealers. They also identified an auto-body shop in Phoenix which was evidently being used as a "stash" house for the weapons after their initial purchase but before they were loaded into vehicles for delivery across the border. Unfortunately, the agents building the Phoenix case could not establish surveillance in a manner that would allow them to see guns being transferred or parked into a particular vehicle within the stash house and therefore weren't able to determine which, if any vehicles were being used to transport the contraband weapons to Mexico. Like the Tucson operation, *Fast and Furious* from the beginning strained the ability of the ATF to conduct any reasonable degree of surveillance, hence creating gaps in information-gathering which compromised the entire operation.

Not only was the ATF allowing guns to walk out of gun shops in and around the Phoenix area, but they also tried to prevent other agencies from stopping straw-bought guns from being sent to end-users both in the United States and Mexico. On November 20, a squadron of Mexican soldiers stopped a truck that had crossed the border at Naco, Sonora, and seized more than 40 AK-47s and a large quantity of ammunition that had been purchased in Phoenix-area shops. The driver of the truck was interviewed by agents from the Immigration Service but refused to talk, and before he could be interviewed further, ICE received a message from the ATF advising them to "stand down" because further questioning might "compromise" an ongoing investigation. This ongoing investigation was so thorough that some of the rifles seized at Naco had been purchased by straw-buyers whose identities until that time were unknown by the ATF.

On December 3 the ATF actually observed a straw sale being conducted in a gun shop for the first time, which was followed by moving surveillance that might have detailed the actual transmission chain being used to move the guns from Phoenix to Mexico. On this occasion ATF and local law enforcement agents observed a known straw-purchaser buying 20 AK-47 rifles and loading them into his truck. He then proceeded to the auto-body stash house where it was finally possible to watch the transfer of these guns to a second vehicle in the parking lot outside the shop. Had the ATF interdicted the activity at this point they would have possessed bona fide evidence of a straw purchase, because the weapons were no longer in the possession of the individual who had filled out the 4473 and carried the guns out of the gun shop. Instead, they followed the second vehicle out of the auto-body parking lot and lost contact with it in a nearby residential neighborhood. Sound familiar?

The motivation on the part of the ATF to expand the gun-running activities of Fast and Furious were not, however, just tied to gathering more evidence about an organized gun-trafficking operation on both sides of the border. It had as much to do with the efforts of the ATF to persuade the Justice Department to approve a Title III wiretap, which had never been previously granted in cases involving alleged violations of gun laws. A Title III tap is a very expensive proposition, involving significant amounts of manpower, electronic resources and costs. Generally speaking, such wiretaps are only granted for major drug or racketeering cases involving high-profile targets, à la John Gotti. Getting approval of a Title III wiretap for a gun case would have vaulted the ATF into a top tier position in federal law enforcement and given the agency a much higher level both of visibility and credibility within the federal law enforcement hierarchy.

DOJ wasn't about to approve a Title III wiretap, however, just to catch a bunch of low-level jack-offs moving some guns from one vehicle to another in the parking lot of an auto-body shop. The ATF would have to demonstrate that electronic surveillance of such activities could lead to the identification and arrest of gun-running entrepreneurs whose business activities were sustaining a real criminal empire that posed an overwhelming threat to public safety on both sides of the border. The 450+ guns that the ATF had walked out of one dealer's shop in *Wide Receiver* was hardly enough to prove the existence of a vast criminal enterprise based on the illicit trade of weapons. This time around, the agency had to make sure that the illegal sales involved multiple dealers and enough weapons to be seen as the workings of an organized, gun-running empire.

In order to have a crime empire, you need a crime boss. And the crime boss who allegedly ended up at the top of this entire volcano was a twenty-four-year-old Mexican national, Manuel Celis-Acosta, whose house in Phoenix was believed to be a stash house for guns and ammunition that would be taken to Mexico, and who had started appearing in various straw transactions within a month after *Fast and Furious* was begun. The first time that Celis-Acosta hit the ATF radar screen was following the straw purchase of guns by an individual named Sean Steward, who purchased 20 AK-47 rifles on December 8 and then returned later the same day to purchase another 20 AKs which had been delivered to the dealer at the same time that Steward was walking out of the shop with the original 20 guns that he purchased that day.

All of these guns ended up in the residence of Celis-Acosta, who had earlier telephoned the dealer to make sure that the second batch of 20 rifles would be held until Steward could return. For the first time the

ATF now had positively identified a buyer who purchased a whole bunch of AKs with cash, as well as an operator of a stash house whose call to the dealer indicated that he was the one in charge. But the realization that Celis-Acosta was the kingpin of the whole operation didn't emerge until May, 2010, when he was stopped as he was about to cross from the US into Mexico at Lukeville, Arizona, in a car that contained less than 100 rounds of ammunition and a small pile of cellphones in a compartment in the dash. Celis-Acosta was detained in Lukeville until the agent in charge of *Fast and Furious*, Hope MacAllister, arrived to question the suspect.

It's important to know that by this time the Title III wiretap had been approved and the ATF was about to submit a request for an extension of the electronic surveillance. And while the ATF had plenty of information regarding the actual straw sales, what they still needed was to link these sales to the Mexican drug cartels in order to show that they were hot on the trails of a vast, criminal enterprise involving the straw purchase of guns. And this link was finally provided for them by Celis-Acosta, who told MacAllister that he was smuggling guns to a major drug cartel in Mexico, and even gave her the name of the cartel kingpin who was, in turn, providing the cash.

At which point in the discussion, MacAllister asked Celis-Acosta whether he would continue to serve as an ATF informant. Guess what Celis-Acosta said? What would you say if you were standing there on the U.S.-Mexico border next to your car filled with contraband and an American law enforcement officer asked if you would agree to work on the agency's behalf? You would say exactly what Celis-Acosta said, which was "yes." And you would then promise, as Celis-Acosta promised, to "keep in touch." And you would then get back into your vehicle and drive off to Mexico, which is exactly what Celis-Acosta did. And would you then "keep in touch?" Of course not. And neither did Celis-Acosta, even though Agent Hope MacAllister took the trouble to write her phone number on a ten-dollar bill, although we don't know whether Celis-Acosta or the ATF supplied the bill.

So here we have the man identified as the *Numero Uno* of a vast criminal empire conducting thousands of straw sales and transporting the guns back to the Mexican drug cartels, who agrees to "keep in touch" by calling a phone number written on the back of a ten-dollar bill, and this is how the ATF conducts this entire affair. Celis-Acosta continued to move guns between the U.S. and Mexico, he continued to frequent his own home in Phoenix, he continued to operate in tandem with other straw purchasers during the remaining months of 2010. He was finally arrested and charged after Agent Terry was killed and *Fast and Furious* was hastily shut down, but he was charged only with smuggling guns into Mexico and at no time was any evidence produced that he was some kind of kingpin running a vast criminal empire involving the straw sales of guns.

But while Celis-Acosta may not have been the valued target that the ATF pictured him to be in their *Fast and Furious* investigation, he was, as it turns out, a valued asset to the FBI and DEA, for whom he was serving as a confidential informant during the same period of time that he was allegedly running his criminal empire that was being investigated by the ATF. And it also turned out that the information about Celis-Acosta's alleged drug cartel connections that the ATF gleaned from their precious Title III wiretap had previously been given to the ATF from another state-level wiretap that had been conducted on Celis-Acosta by the DEA.

You're probably thinking that I'm making this all up. But I'm not, and the reason that much of this information escaped public scrutiny was that when the *Fast and Furious* scandal broke, the politicians who chased it went after bigger political game and, in the process, once again let the ATF off the hook. In this case the bigger political game was Attorney General

Geoffrey Holder and his boss in the White House, the latter who of course knew nothing, the former who initially blurted out a silly little lie and then began furiously back-peddling as the scope of the scandal and the misdeeds of an agency under his control came into full view. But once Holder said he didn't know anything and then had to admit that maybe he knew *something*, the Republicans smelled blood and what should have been a serious and sober discussion about the failings of a government agency became, instead, the usual public donnybrook of partisan accusations, counter-accusations, name-calling and the like.

Meanwhile, what really happened was that between March, 2006 and December, 2007, the ATF observed and/or recorded the straw sales of 474 guns from the inventory of one dealer and made no effort to either stop any of those sales from taking place, nor interview any of the straw purchasers following any of those sales. The agency later claimed that it "seized" 64 of those guns, but those seizures took place in law enforcement actions that were unrelated to the sales and were the work, for the most part, of other law enforcement agencies. The 474 guns were purchased for slightly more than $265,000, and there might have been additional guns that were purchased from that dealer but were not reported as straw transactions. This was the whole shebang known as *Wide Receiver*.

The same ATF agent, William Newell, who had done such a brilliant job of conducting *the Wide Receiver* program between 2006-2007, was then placed in charge of *Fast and Furious,* which started in October, 2009 and was shut down immediately after Brian Terry's death in December, 2010. The former operation covered 19 months while the latter program was conducted for 14 months. Even though *Fast and Furious* was in existence for five months less than *Wide Receiver,* the ATF had evidently learned enough about operations and tactics that they were able to greatly expand the scope and pace of the operation, to wit, more than 2,000 guns were walked out of multiple gun shops during *Fast and Furious*, with the total revenues accruing to dealers in excess of 1.5 million dollars.

And what did all this increased sales activity, dealer involvement and movement of cash in *Fast and Furious* yield to the ATF? Basically the same thing that was gleaned from *Wide Receiver*, namely, a bunch of straw purchases of guns which then went wherever the guns went. Period. No crime empire, no criminal enterprise, no machine shop converting semi-auto rifles into machine guns, no connections to the Sinaloa or other Mexican drug cartel. No nothing.

At one point several of the gun dealers began to get a little queasy about their involvement in this caper, given the fact that although they were making quick dough on this deal, they were also engaging in a lot of illegal sales. Ultimately one dealer had a meeting with Phoenix ATF Supervisor David Voth, who assured them that they would not be held liable for any of the illegal sales, even though he could not actually deliver a formal statement or letter to them expressing these views officially on behalf of the ATF. And the reason he couldn't give them formal assurances was that the relationship between the *Fast and Furious* dealers and the ATF did not exactly conform to the agency's own guidelines for relationships with confidential informants, because such guidelines required that an informant could only commit an illegal act if it was authorized in advance by the agency and was necessary to help fulfill an ongoing criminal investigation.

In fact ATF guidelines did allow agents to observe straw sales without immediately interdicting the movement of the guns, as long as the actual firearms could be traced to the individual or individuals for whom the guns were actually being bought. Not only did this rarely, if ever occur, but there were also instances in which unobserved straw sales took place at gun shops because the ATF agents arrived too late. On several occasions, dealers received calls from straw purchasers asking whether certain inventory was available for purchase, and the dealer indicated the guns could be picked up, then contacted the ATF whose agents showed up as the straw purchasers were pulling away from the dealer's shop with their guns.

I can just see it now. Here I am sitting in my gun shop and I get a call from someone who asks whether the 30 lower receivers he ordered have arrived. Yep, I answer, they're right here, they just came off the UPS truck. Okay, the voice on the other end of the line responds, I'll be right over to pick them up. So I click off the phone, call the ATF office with whom I have been cooperating in making these straw sales, and tell them that the buyer is on his way to pick up the guns. And I know what they are going to say to me: hold him there until we arrive. So a few minutes later the guy shows up, cash in hand. What am I supposed to do? Maybe I should tell him that I've run out of 4473 forms but I have sent someone to another dealer to pick up a fresh supply. Or maybe after filling out the 4473 I'll call the NICS and pretend that I can't get through. Or maybe I'll do this or I'll do that until the ATF boys come stomping in the front door. Now let me interject a reality check at this point. Do you think, dear reader, that there's the slightest chance that the guy who just bought a pile of lower AK receivers wouldn't be able to spot or smell this bunch of ATF as they walked in the door? I mean—give me a break.

The selling pace of *Fast and Furious* as compared to *Wide Receiver* also needs to be understood. The latter operation lasted 19 months, produced 474 verified gun sales for an average of 25 straw-purchased guns per month. In the former operation, roughly 2,100 guns were transferred from dealers to straw purchasers in 14 months, or an average of 125 guns per month. I don't think that more than 10% of all retail gun dealers sell 125 guns of *all* types in a month, never mind just 125 AK-47s and AR-15s. My shop, for example, which sold around 1,000-1,500 guns each year between 2002 and 2014, probably sold a total during those 13 years of 750 assault weapons, or roughly 60 per year, and these dealers in the Phoenix area were unloading that many straw-sale black guns every couple of weeks. With all due respect to the unfortunate and tragic death of Brian Terry, did the ATF actually believe that they could keep this volume of gun sales secret for very long?

The reason the ATF couldn't locate a kingpin who was masterminding the illegal movement of all those guns is because the agency never addressed the simple fact that it was its own intervention in this entire business that allowed the illegal movement of large quantities of weapons to take place. Had they interdicted the original straw purchasers in Tucson in 2006 and again in Phoenix in 2009, the illegal transfer of guns from the U.S. to Mexico would have no doubt continued, but it would have been a sporadic, low-level affair that would have involved a much smaller quantity of contraband guns. The ATF could have sent an advisory around to all Arizona gun dealers alerting them to be more watchful in the case of multiple rifle sales, it could have requested that dealers contact them whenever someone attempted a multiple-rifle sale, or it could have done what it finally did after the *Fast and Furious* mess came to light and instituted a reporting requirement for the same-day purchase of more than two assault-style rifles in gun shops located in states that border Mexico. The agency could have easily instituted any or all of these procedures, but it instituted none.

If you examine the history of the ATF over the last twenty years, read the annual reports, and look at the information they publish which explains what they do and how they do it, one thing stands out above all. The ATF proclaims itself to be the agency that stands on the front lines of fighting gun trafficking which, admittedly, is a threat to public safety and public security. But there's only one little problem. The largest and most dangerous gun trafficking operation ever discovered by the ATF was their own gun trafficking operation, which started in 2006, was suspended in 2007 and then was restarted in a different location in 2009. And the ATF controlled this gun trafficking operation from end to end. Stop and think about what they did.

First, they developed a ready source of supply by inducing a group of legal dealers under their regulatory control to acquire the types of weapons that could easily be trafficked and re-sold. Then they got these dealers to invest more and more money in the purchase of inventory, knowing that they would immediately recoup their investment because nothing would be done to interdict or prohibit these obviously illegal sales from taking place. You can't tell me that those straw purchasers were taking hundreds of assault rifles out of the same shops month after month without any consequences whatsoever and didn't at least vaguely suspect that something a little queer was going on. But their illegal activities, it turned out, weren't being protected by some big gun-running kingpin who worked for the Sinaloa Cartel. The kingpin was actually the ATF, which created a massive gun trafficking operation that could not have succeeded for as long as it did without being organized, managed and led by the ATF itself. Here's a summary of the ATF's gun trafficking activity supplied by the congressional committee which, as it turns out, bungled the investigation of *Fast and Furious* just as certainly as the ATF bungled its operation:

As part of the investigation, ATF relied heavily on support from cooperating Federal Firearms Licensees ("FFLs"). Sometimes, these gun dealers would inform ATF when suspected straw purchasers entered their stores to acquire weapons. On other occasions, ATF would alert the FFLs in advance that straw purchasers were heading to their stores and requested that the FFLs stock up on certain models of firearms.

United States Congress, House Committee on Government Oversight and Reform & Senate Judiciary Committee, "Fast & Furious: The Anatomy of a Failed Operation – Part I of III," July 31, 2012, p. 6.

The problem in all of this bungling goes back to a basic assumption of law enforcement, which presumes there is some kind of connection between controlling crime and controlling guns. I guess this has to do with the fact that criminals, almost by definition, carry and occasionally use guns. Which means that when cops go out to chase criminals, they might find themselves coming up against a gun. The preamble to GCA68 states this explicitly, insofar as it is the government's role to control guns in order to help "officials in their fight against crime and violence." In fact, you can find the same language in the original gun control act of 1938.

There's only one little problem. Since the police, like all good civil servants, want you to overlook the fact (no fault of their own, by the way) that they don't apprehend a majority of the people who commit crimes, at the very least the public should appreciate and understand the difficulties inherent in the job that they do perform. And what makes their job more difficult? All those guns. And if your law enforcement job pertains only to guns, then you really have to remind everyone about the existence and danger posed by all those guns.

So the cops have a funny way of always making a big deal out of guns. Here's a recent example from New York City where a dolt named Elvin Payamps was overheard making threatening comments about "killing cops" while standing on a line at a local bank in Queens. One thing led to another, the guy was arrested after leaving the bank, and the cops allegedly found enough marijuana in his car to get a search warrant for his home, where they turned up what NYPD referred to as an "arsenal" of guns. And since this incident occurred very shortly after two NYPD officers were brutally assassinated while sitting in their squad car on a Queens street, there was no end to editorializing and back-and-forthing about how an alert police department probably saved the lives of a few more cops. Incidentally, the dolt in question, Payamps, had a long record of assaults, mishaps, and this and that, and probably had been whacked over the head a few times by members of New York's Finest— the usual stuff that goes on between the forces of law and order and the lowlifes with whom the cops, unfortunately, have to spend most of their time.

Anyway, it turns out that this arsenal consisted of two guns—a Mossberg shotgun and a 9mm pistol made by Jimenez Arms. Now I may be something of a purist, but to me a gun "arsenal" is more than two guns. Right now I own around thirty guns and I would consider that a small arsenal by the standards of some other gun guys, but at least it's enough guns that if I want to carry a different handgun every day of the week, it's going to take about three weeks before I have to start repeating myself. But a two-gun arsenal? Especially when one of the guns is a pistol that is such a piece of shit that I'm not even sure it will fire once, let alone twice? And it sure won't fire in the direction that it's aimed, unless you really are pointing it at the broad side of the barn.

Here's another example of a "major" gun trafficking operation that the cops busted up in New York City in April, 2014. The kingpin was some dope named Michael Quick who bought guns down South, drove them up I-95 and, with the help of his wife and two uncles, sold the guns to undercover agents between September and April, during which time the cops purchased 155 guns. The last sale consisted of 25 handguns that netted Mister Quick $20,000 in marked bills, and was, according to the NYPD Chief Bill Bratton, "the largest single sale of firearms ever conducted in New York City by the NYPD's Firearms Investigation Unit."

The cops bought 25 guns, and this was the largest transaction they ever made with a gun trafficker in New York City? The ATF in Phoenix or Tucson wouldn't have even bothered to show up at one of their cooperating *Fast and Furious* dealers if all the guy was transferring was 25 guns. But this is how cops like to portray their efforts to control guns. It's always a big deal, like the case in Georgia where a story made national headlines because the Feds broke up a stolen car ring (I wrote about this case in Volume 1: *Guns for Good Guys, Guns for Bad Guys*) involving hundreds of cars that were driven off streets in New York City and then taken to Savannah for shipment overseas. In addition to the cars, law enforcement also seized drugs that were stashed inside some of them, and also claimed that this gang had sold 180 stolen guns to ATF agents over the previous couple of years. And what was the headline that went out to all the wire services about this big bust? It read: "Feds charge 33 in Georgia gun trafficking case."

What ties all these cases together is the traditional way in which law enforcement agencies talk to the public about guns: it's always a big goddamn deal. And guess which agency makes the biggest goddamn deal out of guns?

CHAPTER 6

WHO REGULATES THE REGULATOR?

What jumps out from reviewing the details of Waco and *Fast and Furious* is not just the degree and extent to which the ATF botched both operations; rather, it is the similarity of circumstances that provoked the decision to mount these operations in the first place. In both instances, starting with the Waco dealer and then the dealer in Tucson, it appears to have been the report that a customer walked into the dealer's shop and attempted to purchase a large quantity of legal firearms which were capable of being converted into guns with automatic-fire capability; i.e., machine guns. Note that in neither investigation did the ATF either make an attempt to determine whether or not a machine shop or other facility even existed that could have been used to alter the guns; they were invited to tour the Branch Davidian's compound and declined; they could easily have obtained a probable-cause warrant to search the auto body shop in Tucson but never considered this option. Instead in both cases they focused on one thing and one thing only, namely, using their authority to trace guns from the initial point of sale in order to determine…exactly what, I don't know.

Not only can't I figure out why the ATF assumed they needed to trace guns beyond the countertop in response to the admittedly suspicious purchase of multiple AR-15s and AK-47s, but I also can't figure out why they assumed that anyone who would purchase a pile of semi-automatic rifles was doing said purchase in order to convert the guns into full-auto mode. The truth is that this entire notion that there's some kind of basic difference between rifles used by the military and rifles used by civilians based on whether the guns fire semi-auto versus full-auto is a myth that has grown up over the years in response to the marketing needs of the gun industry, which has little relevance or even reality to how military-style guns are used. And it's a myth that the ATF, the nation's number one regulator of firearm ownership, seems to have bought without spending one second considering whether the myth had any relationship to reality at all.

Here's how the myth got started: even though the M-16 was initially designed as a semi-automatic weapon that would only deliver a round of ammunition every time the trigger was pulled, the confusion over its firing cycle seeped into the gun world through a combination of design modifications, marketing strategies and political agendas. I'll begin with the last one first. On July 1, 1993, a former client of a San Francisco law firm walked into the firm's offices in downtown San Francisco. Over the next half hour, the former client, Gian Ferri, used two Tec-9 handguns and a Chinese-made 1911 pistol to murder eight people, wound six others, and then commit suicide. Ferri's connection to the firm had ended twelve years earlier and no motive for the attack was ever established. But the episode transformed one member of Congress, Dianne Feinstein, into an ardent crusader on the general issue of gun violence and, in particular, the champion from then until now of legislative efforts to rid America of "assault weapons."

Within a few days after the 101 California Street Shooting, as it came to be known, Dianne Feinstein introduced her assault weapons bill in Congress, which was similar to a bill that had already been introduced in Sacramento. And here is where the confusion began, because the Tec-9 was actually a handgun that had little resemblance to the short-barreled military carbine known as the M-16 in its military configuration or AR-15 in the civilian version, but because the magazine loaded ahead of the trigger, as opposed to pistol magazines which usually loaded in the handgrip behind the trigger, the gun could carry 20 or 30 rounds. So in fact the gun looked more like a rifle with the barrel chopped off than like a traditional pistol, and it was thus easier to refer to it and others of similar design as "assault weapons" rather than getting into the nuances of one specific design or configuration versus another.

Ultimately, the compromise bill that became the ten-year Assault Weapons Ban in 1994 prohibited the production and sale of any handgun which loaded from a magazine that attached outside the handgrip or had a net weight (without ammunition) of 50 ounces or more, and any rifle that had certain cosmetic features found on most military long guns, in particular flash suppressors and metal lugs for attaching a bayonet to the barrel. To a greater or lesser extent the bill copied provisions of a change in import regulations that, beginning in 1989, prohibited import of any gun that was considered not primarily used for "sporting purposes," which the ATF defined as guns which looked like standard assault weapons, such as the Uzi carbine, the AK-47 and the Steyr AUG. Of course the 1989 import prohibition was easily circumvented by American manufacturers who simply imported separate gun parts and then assembled the weapons over here, a practice that continues, with various exceptions (the Israeli company that made the

Uzi, for example, refused to ship parts that could be assembled anywhere but in Israel), up to the present day.

The big issue in the Assault Weapons Ban was not, however, the design of guns. Rather, it was the issue of magazine capacity. And on this score, the law required that no gun, handgun or long gun could be manufactured after 1994 unless it was shipped from the factory with magazines that contained no more than 10 rounds. Which basically meant that virtually all of the large-caliber pistols both imported from abroad or made domestically were no longer capable of firing more than 10 shots without changing magazines, whereas previously some of the pistols took magazines that held as many as 18 rounds, and ditto assault-style rifles like the AR-15, which also were previously sold with twenty and thirty-shot mags.

The 1994 Assault Weapons Ban was the first time since 1934 that the Federal Government passed a law that restricted purchase and use of certain types of small arms. The 1934 National Firearms Law made it difficult, but not impossible, for Americans to own full-auto weapons; the 1994 ban made it legally impossible for Americans to purchase certain specific gun models, as well as to own high-capacity magazines for other guns unless the magazines in question had been manufactured prior to 1994. This gave rise in the gun world to an interesting nomenclature, namely a distinction between what were called "pre-ban" guns, as opposed to "post-ban" guns, the difference having to do with whether a gun came with a high-capacity magazine and various cosmetic features or not. In fact an AR-15 or a Glock 19 that was manufactured in 1995 performed exactly the same way that these two guns performed if they were manufactured in 1993, a distinction which disappeared after the Assault Weapons Ban expired in 2004, except in a few states which elected to maintain the ban at the state level.

But there was one provision of the law that created all kinds of truths, half-truths, quarter-truths and God knows what other kinds of truths among gun owners, and this was a provision which prohibited the manufacture of any semi-automatic weapon that was exactly the same as a full-automatic weapon with a semi-auto sear in place of a full-auto sear. The sear is the little piece of metal which is attached to the trigger, and regulates whether the hammer falls only on one round every time the trigger is pulled, or on multiple rounds. You may recall that when I talked about the Branch Davidians, the ATF was unable to find a single instance of Koresh ordering auto-sears for all those assault rifles he kept buying, which gave rise to the notion that he had built a machine shop to manufacture the auto-sears himself. This turned out to be nothing more than fantasy on the part of the ATF, but it was a fantasy that lived on (and still lives on) in the gun-owning culture; i.e., the idea that the difference between pre-ban and post-ban AR-15s was simply that the pre-ban guns could be turned into full-auto weapons by just taking out one part and dropping in another, whereas the post-ban guns needed to have a lot of machining done in order to fit the full-auto sear into the place where the gun now held a semi-auto sear.

In fact there is something called a DIAS, which stands for Drop-In Auto-Sear and does not require any machining whatsoever. This part can be used in both the pre-ban and post-ban guns, and the difference between the DIAS and a regular sear, which does require a small bit of machining, is that the latter tends to be much more dependable whereas the former might jam on occasion. But over the years it has been floating around that the DIAS would only work in pre-ban ARs whereas the real-deal sear was needed for the post-ban because the manufacturers changed the design somewhat so that the post-ban gun wasn't just a "copy" of a full-auto piece. All of this was nothing but loose talk, and remember that it was right after the 1994 bill that the internet started up and everyone could shoot their mouths off on any subject to an unlimited audience.

But more to the point of our story, the discussions about pre-ban versus post-ban and full-auto versus semi-auto focused everyone's attention on the issue of firing mode and made it easier for the gun manufacturers to develop and spread their own myth about assault rifles to counter the myth being spread by the gun-control crowd. Once Senator Feinstein and other anti-gun politicians made occasional rhetorical slips and used words like "automatic" to describe what were really one-pull, one-shot semi-automatic guns, the other side could and did counter with the notion that military guns were automatic weapons whereas civilian guns were semi-automatic and therefore were no more dangerous than any other type of semi-automatic weapon, regardless of magazine capacity and other features.

The argument over full versus semi-auto reached a fever pitch after the Aurora theater shooting in 2012, followed by Newtown in 2013. In both episodes the shooters used high-capacity, semi-automatic AR-15 rifles, with resultant level of death and injury that probably could not have been delivered had they been using only semi-automatic pistols and certainly not with more traditional bolt-action or lever-action rifles. The industry responded to the not-unexpected ramping-up of anti-assault rifle rhetoric by ramping up a campaign of its own, namely, to promote the idea that the AR-15 sold to civilians was something they called a "modern sporting rifle," whose antecedents were, in fact, no different than every other sporting rifle owned by sport shooters and hunters, all such weapons having allegedly started out as military guns that were then adapted for civilian use. The promoters of this story pointed to the original lever-action gun built by Christopher Spencer, which was delivered in small quantities to the Union Army in 1864 and became the design prototype for the Winchester repeater that gained fame in the Indian Wars during the Western settlement, but was also a favored weapon for buffalo hunters and other plains settlers. The same military-civilian small arms transition was claimed to have occurred with early bolt-action rifle designs and thus, the transition from M-16 to AR-15 was right in line with the usual manner in which gun design first embraced military weapons and then moved into the civilian market.

The only problem with this less-than-accurate historical record was that there was no real difference in lethality between the Spencer rifle carried by Federal troops during the Civil War and Spencer rifles carried by trappers and hunters on the frontier. Ditto with bolt-action rifles which, whether they were being aimed at an enemy soldier or a twelve-point buck, still required the shooter to manipulate the bolt action between every shot. But in the case of the transition from the M-16 to the AR-15, the proponents of the modern sporting rifle myth had to deal with the fact that the ordnance delivery of the military gun was at the rate of 600 rounds per minute, whereas the AR-15 could only deliver a round as quickly as the shooter could squeeze off individual shots. Which was exactly what the gun industry touted as being the difference between the military assault rifle and the civilian modern sporting rifle; namely, that one was full-auto and the other a standard, semi-auto gun.

All fine and well except for one little thing. Most of the M-16 rifles delivered to the U.S. Military from the 1960's until today operated in semi-automatic mode. This was due to two factors. First, it was discovered through testing that the excessive speed of the 5.56 NATO round created high levels of friction in the barrel, which in turn heated the barrel to temperatures that impeded the working of the gun. Second, the recoil from full-automatic firing made the gun basically inaccurate beyond the 2nd or 3rd shot, to the point that firing a whole magazine in full-auto mode was basically a waste of ammunition and meant that the shooter was exposed to incoming fire while he was standing there aiming his gun at everything except the enemy combatant. The value of the M-16 was its lightweight, adaptable frame, its accuracy in single-shot mode, and with a short barrel and collapsible stock the fact that it weighed little more than many full-size pistols. It was and is a very good gun for close-contact, mobile deployment of troops, but its value had nothing to do with the gun's ability to deliver full-auto ordnance.

The reason I have discussed this issue of full-auto versus semi-auto at such length is that the confusion over this problem seems to have, first and foremost, existed at the ATF. And the reason for this confusion is that it was the agency's ability to create concern about the straw purchase of assault-style rifles that allowed them to stretch what should have been a simple investigation into possible illegal sales at the countertop into major gun-running conspiracies that were producing or might be producing machine guns whose existence would have posed a serious threat to public safety, no questions asked. The 1993 search warrant that Agent Garcia received in Waco was almost wholly justified on the basis of totally unfounded rumors that the Branch Davidians were manufacturing or assembling full-auto guns. The conscious decision of ATF agents to allow thousands of guns to be illegally sold in Tucson and Phoenix gun shops between 2006 and 2010 was based on the same assumption, namely, that somewhere in both cities guns were being dropped off and converted from semi-auto to full-auto mode. Behind both of these dumb justifications lay the unquestioned myth promoted by the gun industry that there really was one type of weapon for the military and another type of weapon for civilians, and that the bad guys would do anything to trade in the latter for the former. And who, above all, bought this myth hook, line and sinker? The agency that was responsible for regulating an industry whose products this agency didn't evidently understand at all.

Not only didn't ATF personnel know much about the guns whose sales they were allegedly regulating, they also didn't seem to know much about the law under which all this regulating activity was supposed to take place. Because if you look at the GCA68, the government's ability to determine whether any firearms transaction was legal; i.e., a transaction which took place between either dealers and/or consumers who were not prohibited from owning guns, stopped at the point of the transaction. There was nothing in the law that authorized or even hinted at the possibility that the ATF could attempt to trace the movement of a firearm beyond the first transaction, nor did the law explicitly or implicitly allow law enforcement agencies to ask the ATF to conduct such investigations.

Note this statement from the ATF about its National Tracing Center: "ATF's National Tracing Center (NTC) is the only organization authorized to trace U.S. and foreign manufactured firearms for international, Federal, State, and local law enforcement agencies. Its purpose is to provide investigative leads in the fight against violent crime and terrorism and to enhance public safety." The ATF then goes on to say, rather disingenuously, that "the Gun Control Act recognized the importance of firearms tracing in criminal investigations and established mandatory record keeping requirements for persons and entities engaged in the business of dealing in firearms. The Act *led* [my italics] to the establishment of the Bureau of Alcohol, Tobacco, Firearms and Explosives' (ATF) National Tracing Center."

To begin, the GCA68 did not recognize the importance of firearms "tracing" at all beyond knowing who bought a gun from a particular dealer. The GCA68 "led" to the establishment of the National Tracing Center because the ATF created it; there was nothing in GCA68 that mandated or even mentioned it. The only trace that the ATF could perform under GCA68 was to verify the identity of the person who filled out the 4473 form at the initial point of sale. The GCA68 didn't even give the ATF the authority to chase after that individual if it turned out that he lied on the form and shouldn't have received the gun. The GCA certainly didn't give the ATF the authority to chase after that individual to see if he, in turn, sold the gun to someone else. And even if he did sell the gun to someone else, who was to say, as Justice Scalia pointed out during the oral arguments in Abramski vs. U.S., whether the person who initially purchased the gun intended to sell that gun to a third party before he made the purchase?

It's worth repeating the actual commentary by Scalia on this point: "Why is [a straw sale] any more horrible than the notion that as soon as I buy it, I walk out of the store and I meet this guy in the parking lot, he says, 'Hey, that's a nifty looking gun there. How much did you pay for it?' He says, 'You know, I paid 600.' 'I'll give you 700.' 'Oh, it's yours.' Right? I can hand it to him, can't I? So the notion that the gun would somehow get into the hands of somebody who, you know, who wasn't registered or who couldn't buy it himself, that's going to happen anyway."

But all of these concerns could be swept aside if the ATF wasn't just looking for any old kind of gun that might be sold in a parking lot, but was hot on the trail of the most fearsome kind of weapon, namely, a full-auto gun. Which is what they claimed they were doing at Waco in 1993, a claim which turned out to be totally bogus, as was the repeat performance and same claim made in Arizona between 2006 and 2010.

Let me give you a personal example of how the ATF goes out looking for illegally transferred guns. We sold a single-shot old shotgun several years ago. The gun could only fire one shell at a time and then had to be manually reloaded by breaking open the breech and loading another round. I think we sold it to a twenty-two-year-old kid for fifty bucks. Or maybe forty bucks. Or maybe I just gave him the damn thing because he bought a box or two of shotshells. The kid filled out the 4473 and when I called the FBI, he was placed on a three-day delay. But since he lived in the next town over, maybe five or six miles away, it was no big deal for him to come back after the three-day delay had expired to pick up the gun.

In fact he came back on the fourth day following the initial sale, and since we had heard nothing from NICS, under the law I could and did release the gun. Several hours after the happy kid walked out of the store with his newly purchased piece of junk, the NICS called back and said the sale had been denied. The gun's already left the store, I told the NICS examiner, to which she replied okay, call your local ATF office and they'll tell you what to do. Since at that moment I got busy with something else, I asked one of the guys who was working with me in the store that day to make the call. And it just so happened that the guy who made the call on my behalf was a full-time local cop who helped me out from time to time. So he called the ATF and told them that he was a full-time, sworn officer and would go out and retrieve the gun. To which they responded, "Oh no, we'll go out and get it."

So here was a full-time police officer who had bona fide proof that someone was walking around with a gun who was disqualified from owning one and was therefore a clear threat to public safety, and he was being told by the ATF to mind his own business and let them take care of the problem. Except they never took care of the problem. They never went out and retrieved the gun. It wasn't, as the cops like to say, a "priority." It wouldn't lead to a big case involving dangerous guns. Somewhere along the line someone had screwed up in a search on this kid's legal background, forgot to call the dealer and oh well, oh well.

The point about this little anecdote is not to wag a judgmental finger at the ATF. Nor is the point of this entire book to come up with reasons and examples as to why the ATF is no good, or needs to be abolished, or changed, or given more money, or anything else. The point of this book is very simple, namely, to look at the issue of controlling or reducing gun violence and gun crime from the perspective of what would really happen if any of the new laws that are being contemplated to reduce gun violence would actually be put into effect. Because if we expand background checks to cover all private sales, if we make mental health reporting more comprehensive, efficient or both, if we increase regulatory provisions on gun dealers in the hope of weeding out the ones who are "trafficking" all those crime guns, guess which agency will find itself responsible for enforcing all those new regulations? The same agency which right now is responsible for enforcing all current firearms laws. Except there aren't any firearms laws for them to enforce, unless you consider whether someone fills out a form properly is an important law that needs to be enforced or could be enforced.

The truth is that the ATF invented the whole process of gun tracing in the same way that it invented all those full-auto guns being manufactured by the Branch Davidians in Waco or by the straw-purchasers in Arizona who maybe were or weren't working for the Mexican cartels. And as long as the ATF continues to invent what it does instead of sticking to doing what Congress mandated it to do, some guns will move from good hands to bad, and another Waco or *Fast and Furious* will sooner or later occur. If we believe that gun violence is a problem, and some of us do and some of us don't, we need to understand that simply passing another law to reduce gun violence without asking how it will be enforced is really like passing no new law at all.

The only instance of organized, continuous, entrepreneurial gun trafficking that I have found was the gun trafficking conducted by the ATF in Arizona between 2006 and 2010. Think about it. First the ATF ran a beta operation with one Tucson dealer beginning in 2006. Then having learned the ins and outs of the business they created an entire sales network consisting of a group of gun dealers who seemed to have little trouble ordering and receiving hundreds of assault rifles every month. Then they induced these dealers to sell as many guns as they could to certain customers who probably knew, and certainly suspected, that their transactions were being watched. Then they let the customers move the guns from one location to another and eventually sell them to end-users who, in many cases, didn't even live in the United States. So we aren't talking about some penny-ante gun trafficking scheme which takes place between, say, a gun shop in Northern Virginia and some clown doing business on a street corner in Washington, D.C. We are talking about a real, international smuggling ring which was only shut down when a couple of pissed-off ATF agents blew the whistle on the whole shebang. If Border Patrol Agent Brian Terry had not been gunned down in December, 2010, was there any reason why the gun trafficking activity of the ATF wouldn't still be going on?

Before this volume comes to a close, I'd like to make a brief point about black guns and "crime guns." When I was a kid growing up in the 50's, there was a clear division in this country between military life on the one hand and civilian life on the other. There was a universal draft which snagged most able-bodied men for two years of active service, and while you were in you were in, and when you left and were out, you were out. I was born and raised in Washington, D.C., so there were lots of what we called "servicemen" walking around, and the term didn't mean the guy who came to fix the washing machine, it meant someone who was serving in the military. And you could spot them right away because they wore these khaki uniforms which they threw away and never wore again once their term of service was up.

Soldiers not only dressed different from civilians, they also carried different types of guns. The gun they carried in all the parades, and there were plenty of parades in Washington, D.C., was either the old, bolt-action Springfield that was still issued to the troops until the latter part of World War II, or the semi-automatic M-1 Garand. The stocks of these rifles were wood, they were big, heavy, clumsy things, and if you only stood about 5'6", when you hoisted one of these guns on your shoulder, it looked taller than you.

There were also plenty of guns owned by civilians when I was growing up, but they were guns designed for hunting or occasionally sport shooting, and they looked entirely different from the guns I saw soldiers carrying in their parades. The hunting rifles were usually sleek, bolt actions like the Winchester Model 70, which was first produced in the 1930's but was still going strong when I was a kid, or the lever-action Winchester Model 64 whose antecedent, the Model 94, dated back to around the time of the Spanish-American War. Cops carried revolvers, and an occasional high-ranking military man had a holster for the 1911 pistol on his belt, though the gun was usually not carried, or was kept safely tucked inside the flap.

Military and civilian styles began to merge at some point not that long ago, and the first place I noticed the blurring of the two styles was in clothing, when camo prints started to become a fashion statement in all the better stores. If I wanted to wear camo as a kid I went to an Army-Navy store, of which I recall there were a couple of retailers on Canal Street in lower Manhattan whose floor spaces were cluttered with mounds and mounds of pants and shirts, or what we called "fatigues," along with those leather "bomber" jackets which competed with the black, metal-edged motorcycle jackets that Marlon Brando first popularized in the movie *The Wild Ones*, which came out in 1953.

If you were a college student (like I was) in the 60's and you wore military clothing, it was probably because you were on your way to a demonstration against the Vietnam War. Camo and military clothing started out as a political statement but, like everything else in America, a few bright entrepreneurs realized that all those long-haired protestors were going to grow up to be middle-class citizens with plenty of spendable cash to spare. So camo became a fashion statement along with the cargo pants which replaced jeans, and believe me when I tell you that there were troops in Iraq who sometimes brought their own military-style clothing along when they were deployed because the stuff they were issued didn't look quite as good or fit quite as well.

The second area in which military and civilian styles began to blur was in the design and marketing of small arms. Sometime in the 1980's, the demand for domestic and imported long guns (shotguns and rifles) began to slow down. This was an inevitable consequence of shifting demographics; i.e., the disappearance of the rural population and the concomitant end of hunting as a major outdoor sport. When I was growing up, the term "outdoor sports" meant hunting and fishing, whereas for my children it meant hiking, kayaking and the like. A few years ago the NSSF put out a report that claimed an enormous economic benefit from hunting, except that to calculate the financial impact they utilized sales figures for virtually every type of method that could be used to get from one place to another out-of-doors. I thought it was both laughable and desperate that they claimed the revenues from sales of kayaks as an example of how much money the hunting population was spending on its sport.

The shift away from traditional-style hunting guns to smaller, lighter weapons, both handguns and long guns, was also a consequence of changes in manufacturing technology such as metal-injection molding and polymers, which led to smaller and lighter consumer goods of all kinds, not the least firearms. The virtue of polymer replacing wood stocks, for example, meant that guns could be "tricked out" with all kinds of sights, lasers and optics that not only made the gun more "customized" to fit the personal desires of the owner, but also added a hefty sum to the bottom-line purchase price at the counter-top. Not only did various types of accessories flourish in gun stores, but the internet drove accessory sales in the same way that consumers were now purchasing all sorts of gadgets, electronic and otherwise, through online channels. When I first opened my retail gun store in 2001, one whole wall was devoted to sporting scopes, usually Leupold (expensive), Nikon (moderate) and Tasco (cheap). I stopped selling scopes in 2005-2006 because there was no way I could compete with online sellers like Amazon and eBay, both of whom sold everything related to guns except the guns themselves.

But where military and non-military consumer tastes really began to merge was in the stepped-up militarization of the home front after the 9-11 attacks and the beginning of an unending level of military activity that started in 2002 in Afghanistan and continues (I am writing this in December, 2014) until this day. Granted that the level of engagement, expenditures and casualties is far below those experienced in other American wars. But advances in media, particularly social media, brings every military action home for viewing with an immediacy that never before existed. So the viewer and the battlefield are one and the same, and the weapons that the viewer sees on the battlefield can all be purchased at the local shop.

Which leads me to make a further point. The real problem with the "war on terror" is that the traditional line demarcating the "criminal" versus the "enemy" has disappeared. We no longer think of the "enemy" in military terms; when a crazed-out kid can tote a bomb into Times Square or the Boston Marathon, then the military and police, like it or not, get morphed into one. This being the case, why shouldn't the gun industry respond by making and marketing products that have as their ultimate rationale the notion of self-defense? When I was a school kid we practiced defending ourselves against the "enemy" by crouching down under our desks and then waiting for the teacher to yell "all clear" following the make-believe nuclear attack. Today school kids are taught how to quickly exit their classroom in the event of a shooter entering the school, and cops work on "quick response" tactics and drills all the time. But remember when Chechen rebels took 1,200 kids hostage and eventually killed several hundred in an assault on a Russian public school? Don't we talk all the time about how something like that could happen here?

Readers of my vintage may remember an Irish gang called the "Westies" that operated out of Hell's Kitchen in New York City and was considered the worst, most vicious gang ever to operate in New York or anywhere else. They were so violent that the Mafia often sub-contracted their mob hits to this bunch, because they enjoyed killing so much that they could be counted on to get the job done. And it wasn't like they had to worry about anyone snitching on them to the cops since most of the neighborhood snitches were members of the gang.

I grew up in a neighborhood in New York whose local gang was reputed not only to be tougher and more violent than the Westies, but whom it was rumored were often the boys who carried out those hits for the Westies that were originally contracts from the mob. None of the members of this gang ever carried guns, because whenever anything went down in the neighborhood, the cops would come around, line them up against a wall, deliver the Miranda warning by bashing them in the face or kicking them in the ass, and then pat all of them down for guns. And if anyone was found in possession of a banger, he was going away for a long time.

The gang's M.O. for taking someone out was to drag the poor bastard up to the top of an apartment building, preferably one that was under construction because then nobody would be around at night, and toss the guy off the roof. So five guys went into the building and four came back downstairs under their own steam. These guys were professionals in every sense of the word. They didn't use guns because guns were for kids, for jerks, and for assholes who created more problems using guns than could ever be solved.

This is the real connection between crime and guns, a connection which has little to do with why most crimes involving guns actually occur. The FBI data on this point is very clear: probably four out of five gun crimes involve perpetrators and victims who had clear and continuous contact before the actual shooting took place. In shootings where women are the victims, which is 15% of all homicides, the domestic connection between these women and the guys who pulled the trigger is virtually one hundred percent. In the case of gun morbidity—injury known as aggravated assault—the degree of pre-incident contact between the shooter and the victim is the same.

When the ATF says that they are the first line of defense against gun crimes, they are creating a category of criminality which doesn't really exist. And while the NRA is correct when they say that people kill people, what they leave out is the fact that the most efficient way for someone to kill someone else is to use a gun. What I am suggesting, and the data backs me up on this score, is that most people who commit "gun crimes" arrive at an impulsive, unplanned moment in which having a gun handy means they can inflict a much greater level of injury, which then turns the use of the gun into a crime. But giving the ATF greater responsibility to monitor the movement of these "crime guns" will do little, if anything, to reduce crime. And buying the ATF's nonsense about this vast, underground commerce in illegal guns controlled by gun-trafficking cartels is to buy their rationale for existence which has little to do with why and how some dopes, jerks and assholes acquire and use guns.

NOTES ON SOURCES

With a few exceptions, all of the sources used for this book are in the public record and most of them are cited in the text. Readers who want to go beyond what I have said or reproduced in my text should consult the congressional sources from whom excerpts have been cited, along with Executive Branch publications from the Department of Justice and the ATF. I also quote many media sources which are obviously taken from online media channels of relevant newspapers, television stations, etc.

As for published sources, there is a vast literature on both Waco and *Fast and Furious*, most of which rehash various conspiracy theories that abound whenever a Democrat (Clinton or Obama) sits in the White House. I can't say that any of these books went far beyond the congressional sources mentioned in the text, but at least Dick Reavis, *The Ashes of Waco—An Investigation* (New York: Simon & Schuster, 1995) is a serious effort and shouldn't end attempts to present the story in an organized, credible way.

The chapters on GCA68 and Abramski are almost entirely built on published SCOTUS documentation, but I also learned a great deal about federal gun control from two academic articles: Frank Zimring, "Firearms and Federal Law: The Gun

Control Act of 1968," *Journal of Legal Studies*, 4, 133 (1975), 133-198; and, David Hardy, "The Firearms' Owners Protection Act: A Historical and Legal Perspective," *Cumberland Law Review*, 17 (1986), 585-682. I thank the author for sending me this and other relevant texts.

ABOUT THE AUTHOR

Michael R. Weisser was born in Washington, D.C., educated in New York City public schools and received a Ph.D. in Economic History at Northwestern University. He is a featured blogger with Huffington Post and also blogs about guns at www.mikethegunguy.com. Since 1978 he has been a firearms retailer, wholesaler, law enforcement distributor and importer with total gun sales in excess of 30,000 handguns, rifles and shotguns. He is also a Life Member of the NRA and a certified firearms instructor in six specialties. He can be reached at his blog or at mike@mikethegunguy.com.